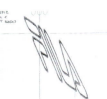

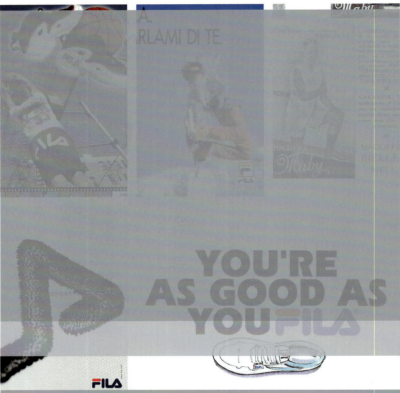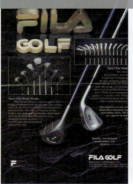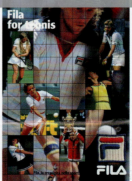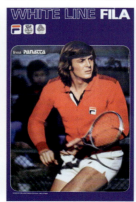

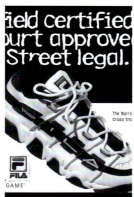

PP. 179–208

PP. 224–236

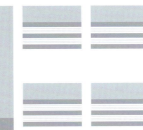

P. 231

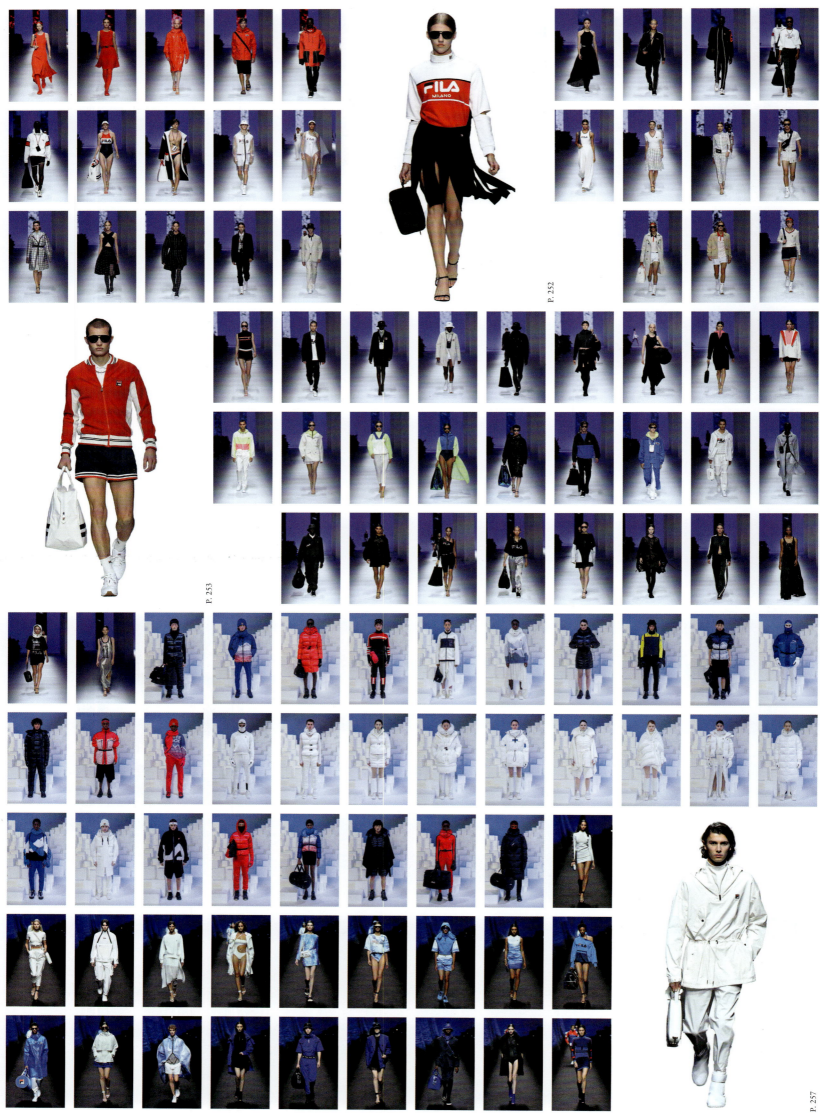

P. 252

P. 253

P. 257

	FOREWORD Silvia Venturini Fendi	13
	INTRODUCTION Angelo Flaccavento	15
Essays	FILA – A STORY BY OBJECTS Marta Franceschini	17
	THE THIN RED LINES Matteo Codignola	61
	MEMORY TEST – ATHLETES AND AMBASSADORS Carlo Antonelli	105
	MODERN TRADITION: A TIMELESS LOGO Emanuele Coccia	149
	"CHANGE THE GAME" – FILA AND THE EVOLUTION OF ADVERTISING FROM THE 1970s TO THE 2000s Michele Galluzzo	177
	CITY GENTS AND FRESH CREWS: FILA'S SUBCULTURAL TRAJECTORIES FROM THE CLAY COURTS TO THE STREET Lorenzo Ottone	221
	FILA: INSIDE AND OUTSIDE FASHION Angelo Flaccavento	249
Fiction	EVERYTHING FALLS Silvia Calderoni	50
	BJÖRN BORG'S POLO Karl Holmqvist	94
	EAGLES, DEVILS, GELATO: THE SECRET HISTORY OF A SHOE Charlie Fox	138
	NOW FOR A STORY THAT BEGINS WITH A CLIFFHANGER Jeffrey Burton	166
	KINGDOM OF DREAMS Rahim Attarzadeh	210
	TO GIOVANNI SOLDINI CB Hoyo	238

FILA: TIMELAPSE

CURATED BY
ANGELO FLACCAVENTO

FOREWORD

When we were kids, my sister and I would spend the summer playing tennis. I wasn't good at it at all, and the afternoons we spent at the sports center seemed endless. However, I do have a vivid recollection of my FILA outfit: it was a must for anyone who played tennis. I was very proud of it. It had something special about it: an aura that the other brands didn't have, amplified by the athletes who endorsed it, the torchbearers of deep values. Although I was just a teenager, my impression of the Davis Cup won in Santiago de Chile in December 1976 by Adriano Panatta and Paolo Bertolucci wearing red FILA polo shirts was that it was a moment of greatness. In a country like Chile, blood-stained by dictatorship, that sign of protest reverberated far and wide: it showed courage and spontaneity, values that have always touched me. Those were years when hedonism and commitment did not exclude each other. After that, FILA continued to accompany me as I grew. Then I inevitably forgot about it, although the feeling and the memories of a special and authentic brand remained. It was in 2018 that FILA came back to mind. Hey Reilly, the digital artist with whom I was collaborating, a skilled manipulator of slogans, logos, and images, created the play on words Fila/Fendi that instantly clicked. That was when our full-fledged collaboration began. The first of its kind for us, and a pioneering one, kissed by the success with the media and the public. Karl Lagerfeld as well, who was generally not fond of these sorts of things, was enthusiastic about the idea from the outset. We used the FILA logo, joined with the double "F" of Fendi, in a very sophisticated way, on jacquard fabrics or knitted onto bags. Nothing of the kind had ever been seen before. For the young, like my daughters, it was a discovery, while for everyone else, it was a rediscovery. What excited me about FILA was not just its authenticity but also its constant desire to try things out, establishing a live and real contact with the public. Which is what this book celebrates: FILA, the first brand to come from a tennis court—whatever the court—to enter life and the collective imagination, in the subcultures as well as the everyday. Always with an unmistakable identity, sealed by the perfect "F" of the logo. I don't think there can be a greater victory in terms of impact and durability in time.

Silvia Venturini Fendi

INTRODUCTION

The story of FILA has lasted for more than a century. Squeezing it into a rigid grid would not have made much sense. There are fundamental dates and junctures, of course; important moments and epic heights. However, the constant flux, the organic movement of ideas and objects is what truly strikes us, always encapsulated in memorable images, or simply brimming with value and meaning. This is what led to the idea of structuring this volume like a visual narrative in an endless loop: a TIMELAPSE that sums up the story of FILA by short-circuits and spatiotemporal leaps.

FILA became part of popular culture, quickly moving beyond the boundaries of the playing field. The athletes were the vehicles and the ambassadors, side by side in the sports competitions, dressed and rising to a level of fame akin to that of a rock star, and a fresh, quick, innovative advertising language. All this unfolds in the pages that follow, with a certain freedom with respect to the actual chronology, but also with the manifest evidence of a documentary record.

The visual tale is interspersed with essays that, like a magnifying lens, enlarge and extrapolate the details of the story and its bearing, exploring the most salient pieces of clothing but also key topics, like the company's association with top tennis players and high-ranking athletes that have contributed to FILA's public success. Analyzed here as well is the logo, a masterpiece of graphic equilibrium and the trigger of affiliations, and there's also the advertising language that is never banal. Lastly, there was no way we could overlook FILA's relationship with the subcultures, as the driver of transgenerational endurance.

The very free manner that FILA has always used to communicate suggests a further experiment, one that is perhaps more abstract but no less meaningful: a series of texts, between the narrative and the poetic, entrusted to artists, writers, and creatives who work with words; free interpretations, rereadings, stories about certain iconic items of clothing with a very long history, and about the people who wore them. These are windows on other possible worlds, the catalyzers of latent meanings, but also pure moments of literary pleasure.

This short introduction, to be viewed as a guide for the reader, is an invitation to approach TIMELAPSE exactly for what it is: a flux that one can enter at any time and from any place. The suggestion is to browse through this book and read its contents in order, following the table of contents, but also skipping back and forth, going here and there. In short, however the reader wishes to: in TIMELAPSE, everything makes sense.

Angelo Flaccavento

FILA – A STORY BY OBJECTS
Marta Franceschini

ROOTS

Before the plot, before the adventures, the ups and downs, and the triumphs, every good story needs two fundamental elements: a time and a place. The "once upon a time in a faraway land" for FILA resides in early twentieth-century Biella. Here, the morphology of the region has defined its identity: the soaring peaks of the Alps, the basin protected by the highlands and cut by the fast-flowing waters that cross it, and then the valleys, the gentle hills, the plains. The variety of the landscapes and the position of "distant proximity" from the cities—Milan, Turin, but also Paris—consequently shape its inhabitants as well, influencing their lifestyles and activities.

So, the natural inclination for contemplation from a privileged vantage point encounters the determination to consolidate the analysis into action-and-reaction: an interesting blend of intuition and a taste for risk-taking that the people of Biella put into practice in various fields, primarily in the textiles sector. Intuition was what, in the early twentieth century, led Giovanni Fila, a member of a family dedicated to woodworking, to learn to repair those textile machines—the symbols and tools of the Italian industrial revolution—which had been significant in Piedmont in the previous century. Meanwhile, the taste for risk-taking was fulfilled in 1911 when Giovanni decided to change the course of the family business and opened a spinning mill for carded and combed wool, setting up factories in Cossato.

Spinning allowed FILA to acquire a knowledge of raw materials and become aware of the techniques and machinery required for actual clothing production. In 1926, the spinning mill became a part of the company's activities, moving further toward the finished product and thus gaining complete control over the supply chain. The establishment of Maby (Maglificio Biellese Fratelli Fila), which produced underwear for women, men, and children, marked the beginning of a growth process that, through domestic cohesion and business developments, market analyses, acquisitions, political skills, and strategic decisions, led the FILA group to a considerable size—around 2,500 workers in the 1960s—with a structure stable enough to stride confidently through a decade characterized by change, and economic as well as social upheaval.

THE TECHNOCRAFT BOOM

The revolutionary spirit of the late 1960s thus drove Fila to reconsider its chosen production category, moving from underwear to outerwear. However, this change did not come about smoothly. All they had at their disposal were circular machines used to manufacture underwear, which presented major technological constraints related to the yarns and counts, color blends, shapes, and details. Those very constraints that were supposed to harness creativity instead set the boundaries within which to explore design possibilities and introduce the company's new course. The company split into two groups to better handle the vertical production cycle, which went from the yarn all the way to distribution.

When, in the transition between the 1960s and 1970s, Giansevero Fila brought Enrico Frachey and other figures outside of the family into the company's management, he did so because he felt the need to respond to the demands of the new society that was taking shape. Economic stability translated into a joyful diversification of interests and a reconfiguration of daily life, with washing machines at home, the excitement of technicolor, and more time for leisure activities. In 1973, Maby became FILA Sport, marking the beginning of an internal technological evolution within the company. This led to the conversion of circular knitting machines adapted for use with more performance-oriented fabrics suited to physical activities. These fabrics embodied the tactile characteristics that were "close to the skin," influenced by a renewed sense of the body—and freedom to explore it through clothing—emerging from the theorizations of social and sexual liberation movements. The item that exemplified this evolution was the polo shirt, made of lightweight *fil d'Écosse*, or cotton thread, buttonless with snap fasteners to prevent fabric snagging, and featuring a soft two-tone collar. A piece of clothing that was suitable for both the playing field and a leisurely Sunday stroll. The product was the result of industrial intelligence and the stylistic attention of Pierluigi Rolando, a self-assured designer with a background as a textile engineer who had trained in Leeds, capable of combining, as he put it, "technique and invention." Since 1971, Rolando has worked with an enterprising team assembled by Fila and Frachey. The team included the technician-cum-creative Alessandro Galliano, the coordinator Gianni Fantini, Felicita de Toma, an exceptional negotiator with third-party producers, Mario Mossa with his strong commercial insight, and lastly, the keen eye of the advertising expert Sergio Privitera.

In particular, Mossa and Privitera tried to answer a key question: how to inform people about the ongoing change? By acting on the image: the evolution thus expanded to the other parts of the company as well, and drove the development of a sophisticated visual language mindful of the directions of fashion communication, Italian and not only that. The images reflected the attention to the publishing materials that were taking root in those years. In that period Italy was indeed a fertile territory for publications that expressed—visually as well—the emotions of a society undergoing transformation: from corporate journals like *Uomo IR* and *TOP* to the experimentations of *L'Uomo Vogue*, founded in 1967 with the clear intention of transferring to the page the enthusiasm of the anti-bourgeois social revolution, the revolution of the young who did not want to dress like their fathers before them, promoting "stylism" as a new methodology that brought together artisanal tradition, technical know-how, and style, capable of intercepting what was desired and translating it into wearable objects.

The stylistic inclination was not only expressed through the products, but through their representation as well, and in the total sublimation of concepts and ideas into symbols, into logos. Privitera studied the historical images of the promotion of FILA and designed the F-Box: extreme synthesis, inspired by the immediate work-slogans of Robert Indiana, maintaining the taste and the cosmopolitan ambitions of the origins, but anchoring FILA to the present, to the hegemony of the people and pop consumerism, nodding to the new tastes and the new markets, and preparing the brand to implement the global affirmation predicted by that historical illustration that shows a large "F" like a flag planted into the ground looming over the world.

BODY STYLES

Changing the game means overturning a paradigm and, in a fixed scenario, imposing a style that modifies its rules. Unsurprisingly, "Change the Game" was the slogan Enrico Frachey had chosen to use in leading FILA to "conquer" the American market. At first, the game primarily changed by introducing "elegance" as a keyword in sportswear design. The first FILA tracksuit that Rolando designed was the expression of the desire to offer versatile clothing suitable for different occasions: a sportswear outfit inspired by the clean and sharp lines of a tuxedo, evoking sophistication that challenged—and defeated—the passing of time.

After making the company "future-proof" in terms of design and production with White Line in 1973, it became clear to the company's management and creatives that what was needed was an innovative marketing strategy that leveraged the recognizability of the FILA logo and products. The idea was therefore to associate FILA with equally recognizable personalities who were leaving their mark in the sports arena, whose global influence impacted players and fans, transforming them into icons and followers, respectively. Following the insight of Paolo Bodo, a consultant and talent scout, as well as a tennis player himself, FILA first approached Nicola Pietrangeli and then Adriano Panatta. Panatta, with his rhythmic, *romano*, and tireless net-attacking style, embodied the new spirit—and non-elitist approach—of contemporary tennis. He became the protagonist of a feature dedicated to FILA that appeared in the pages of *L'Uomo Vogue*, where the player was portrayed "in action," for an intense display of passion and belief, characteristics shared with the brand and the people who were instrumental in idealizing it.

The athlete whose image is linked to FILA more than anyone else's is the Swede, Björn Borg. Frachey contacted Borg in 1975, and Rolando designed a collection specially for him, unveiled in 1976. The collection included a complete outfit featuring a "chalk-striped" polo with vertical stripes accentuating Borg's slender physique, and shorts made of warp-knit jersey (instead of weft-lock, beaten and dense but less resistant to movement and inevitably yielding), with an elastic waistband and side slits. All of these lines exploited the natural elegance of Borg's movements and his tireless and constant playing style. Printing the vertical stripes on crocheted knitwear was a subtle and extraordinary addition: a technical invention by Rolando and the Salussoglia husband and wife team, who managed to impress precise equidistant stripes onto the cut knitwear, leaving the sides white. Once again what the designers envisioned was the visual impact of the polo shirt being swiftly moved over Borg's strong muscles. In 1978, Borg began wearing a shirt featuring two adjacent logos that became one: F-Box and BJ, proof of the indissoluble bond between the brand and its embodiment, erasing the hierarchy between icons that share fame.

Drawing on the athlete—hence on his body but also on his movements, his playing style—was the main characteristic of Rolando's design approach, who along with his wife Lydia, a skilled illustrator, studied male as well as female players and suggested customized solutions for each identity. The solid physique of Guillermo Vilas, the most famous Argentinian tennis player and great rival of Borg on the clay courts, called for a different design that factored in the proportions of the athlete's body, besides his powerful playing style; Rolando decided to emphasize the sides with the insertion of a side panel and some horizontal lines that emphasized the waistline. The versatility of the Australian-Wiradjuri Evonne Goolagong, known as the Sunshine Girl, required an attire that was lively and colorful and that echoed her agile game as she attacked and defended.

The specific attention to the differences in the bodies and their styles went beyond the tennis court and to the other sports that FILA wanted to focus on, implementing a productive and communicative diversification that was always based on the ability to respond to the physical challenges that all the different athletes—tennis players, mountaineers, skiers, swimmers, golfers, yachtsmen—are called upon to face from one moment to the next.

FEATS AND REVIVALS

While continuing to consolidate its presence on grass and clay courts, FILA also moved on other terrains, always focusing on individuals and their feats. After the Italian conquest of Yosemite by the Piedmontese Giorgio Bertone and Renzino Cosson, the FILA group was engaged in developing a snow wear line, at first called Roc Neige and later White Rock, conceived to provide clothing in which aesthetics and technical performance coincided with the "anarchic" approach of the new mountaineering, represented in those days by Reinhold Messner. Care and respect for the mountain were the values that Messner wanted to be expressed in his outerwear, and for this reason the mountaineer collaborated with Rolando to infuse the constructive details of the clothing with experience, from the perfecting of the four-pocket jacket made from sailcloth to the study of a sweater with sides that open, from the harmonization between the colors and the nuances of the mountain to the use of ergonomic and high-performance materials. Solutions and strategies also used in the skiwear lines: for Ingemar Stenmark's Swedish Alpine ski team padding that was part of the ski suit was tested from the late 1970s, an innovation that would be put on the market in 1981.

From the mountain to water, 1976 saw the launch of the swimwear collection; the first participation in the world of sailing took place in 1977. The development of the swimwear line Aqua Time called for a totally new study of the environmental conditions that the athletes found themselves in, and clearly also of the movements and the resistance for which the materials and the designs needed to adapt. The friction of the water was offset by the "eggshell" patent: an elastic material with a smooth surface, made at the behest of the swimmer Marcello Guarducci and popularized by Giovanni Franceschi, who competed at the 1984 Los Angeles Olympics wearing a figure-hugging swimsuit—one size smaller than his own, to guarantee grip and performance—as always designed by Rolando. As regards sailing, after the sponsorship of Luciano Ladavas and Pierre Sicouri's *Guia IV* and of Antonio Chioatto's *Traité de Rome*, FILA supported the Azzurra consortium for the America's Cup in 1987. Subsequently, the brand supported the feats of Giovanni Soldini, with whom it would start collaborating in 1996. Soldini's contribution was essential to the advancement of the stylistic and productive research not only as concerned the practical details of the competitive sailing uniform, but also the sustainable materials, encouraging the company to think creatively and consciously about its own effect on all those areas, from snow-capped peaks to the open sea, where FILA was and is present.

In the field of sports, competition in its various forms lay down the directions that FILA took, not only in terms of research and production but also in terms of style: the perfect channel through which to address a less specialized but nonetheless enthusiastic audience. FILA did not limit itself to professionals but also conquered a broader public, with trendy ideas appreciated by amateurs as well. In this sense, women's swimsuits played a key role in communication—from one-piece suits with vertical lines and a large logo on the back, to single-shoulder designs with a white base and flames spreading out toward the center. Swimsuits that wrap around the statuesque bodies of fashion models, characterizing FILA's visual fashion statement: *power, rhythm, and style*, as stated in the 1976 ad for the Aqua Time line.

The "feats" most tied to the expression of the fashion brand can be traced back to Čedomir Komljenović, an image-maker who worked on permeating the FILA imaginary with the key stylistic features of the 1980s: saturation, spectacle, and sex. In his photographs, just as in the events staged in St. Moritz, the Waldorf Astoria of New York, and Monte Carlo, Komljenović appears capable of imbuing every phenomenology of the brand with a bold, joyful, international taste.

DEFINING IS REDEFINING
Internationalization also marked the managerial direction that the brand took from 1983 onward, when a new industrial structure and new challenges emerged, mainly related to a focus on footwear production. Manufactured under license by the Lario shoe factory, located not far from Milan, the commercial success of FILA shoes was due to Homer Altice, who succeeded in placing FILA sports shoes in Foot Locker stores. The work group consisted of Kevin Crowley and Jack Steinweis, in charge, respectively, of style and its transformation into a product. Gene Yoon was head of financing and production, and, once again, Enrico Frachey returned in 1987 after a hiatus of a few years to redefine the FILA lexicon for the developing market.

Frachey remained faithful to the strategy perfected in 1973 and chose the rising basketball star Grant Hill of the Detroit Pistons as brand ambassador—or rather, once again, as the embodiment—of FILA 95, known back then as the Grant Hill 1. Ambition and appropriation are sentiments inherent in the configuration of street style: the rapper Tupac Shakur became an "accidental" endorsement for the transition from the basketball court to the streets. Shakur popularized "Functional Fashionable Formidable" shoes like the GH2 with their logoed sole, paving the way to yet another reconfiguration of the FILA spirit, which since then has been expressed in distinctive shoes, first and foremost the Disruptor. The first model appeared in 1996 and since then it has remained one of the most recognizable items in the brand's conversion into street-casual style.

In addition to consolidating its omnipresence in sports—from tennis to sailing, from basketball to golf, from athletics to rowing, from skiing to motorsports, and even football, and the list could go on and on—FILA's umpteenth new direction, starting in 2007 with the acquisition by Gene Yoon, demonstrates a clear design awareness that creates a seamless connection between leisure, lifestyle, and fashion. FILA, and above all its historical heritage of inventions and reinventions, technical innovations, and stylistic propositions, opens up to a synergistic dialogue with external identities. Anna Sui, Jason Wu, Gosha Rubchinskiy, Glenn Martens, Silvia Venturini Fendi, Roksanda Ilinčić, Haider Ackermann are just a few of the designers who have recently been invited to become enamoured with the brand's history and write new chapters for its future.

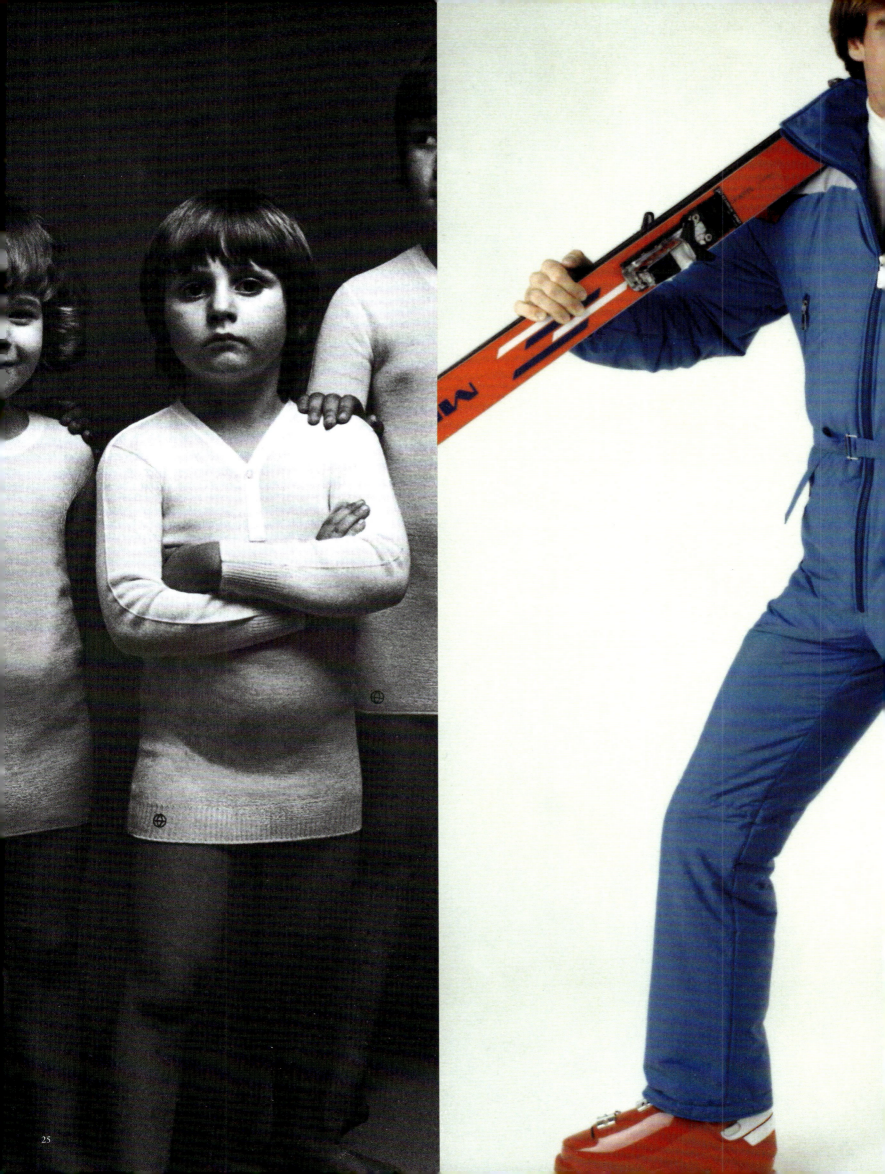

RODI

1

2

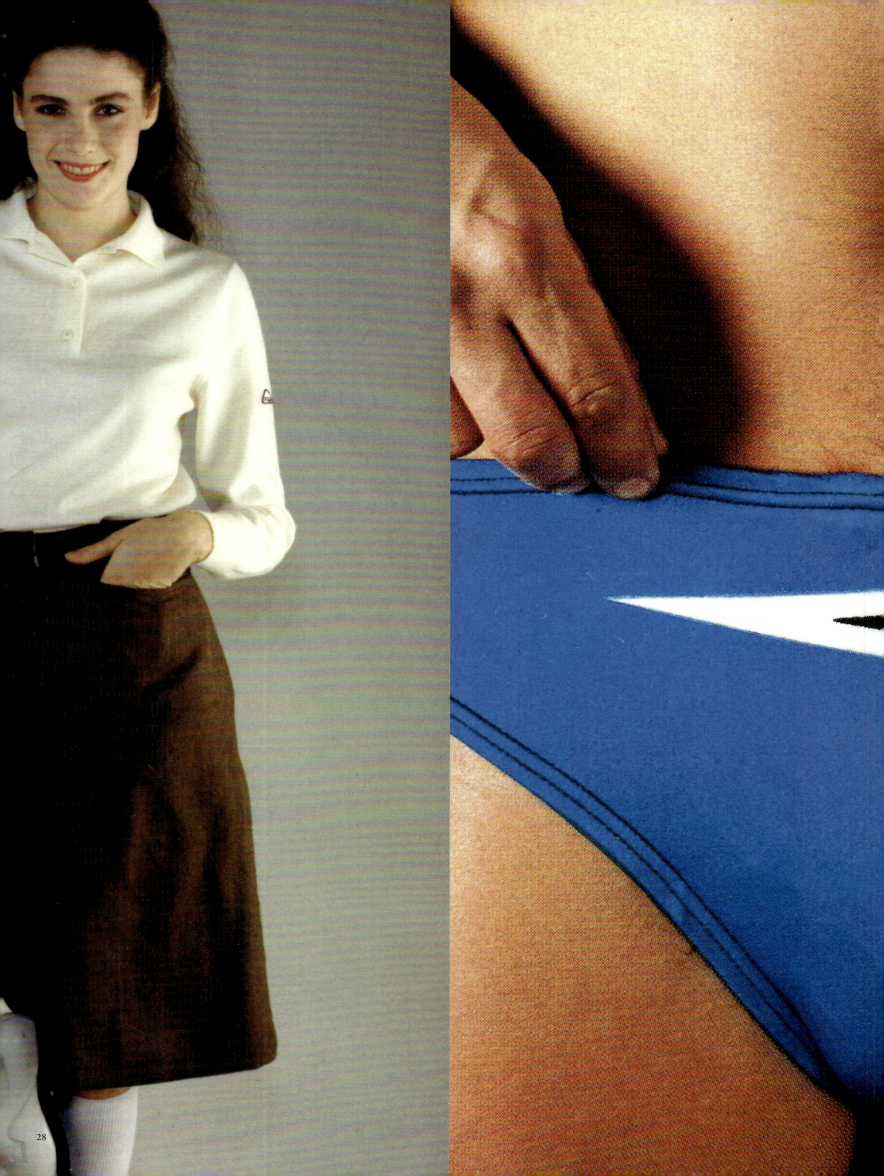

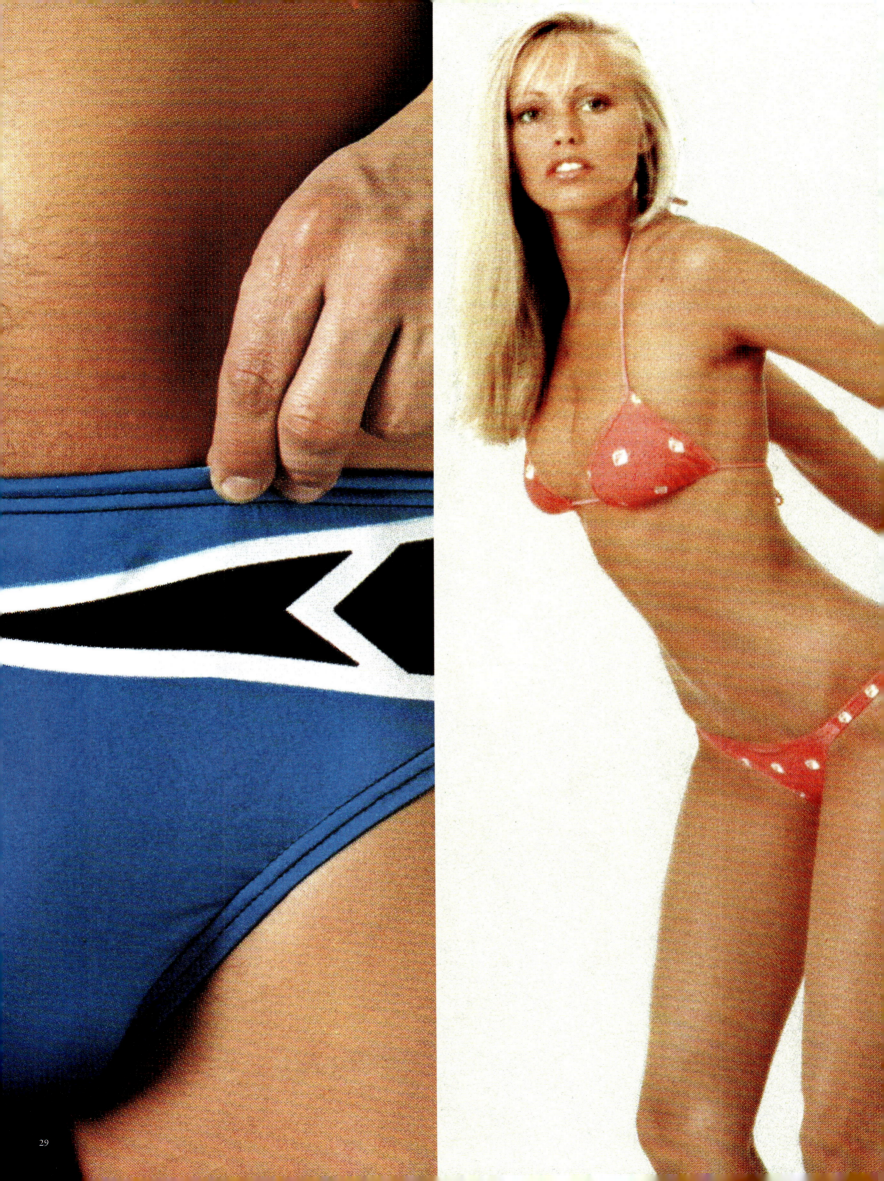

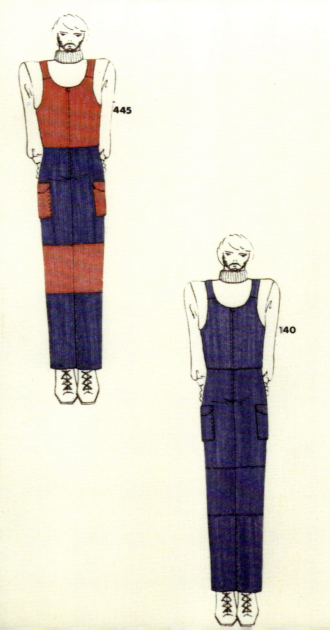

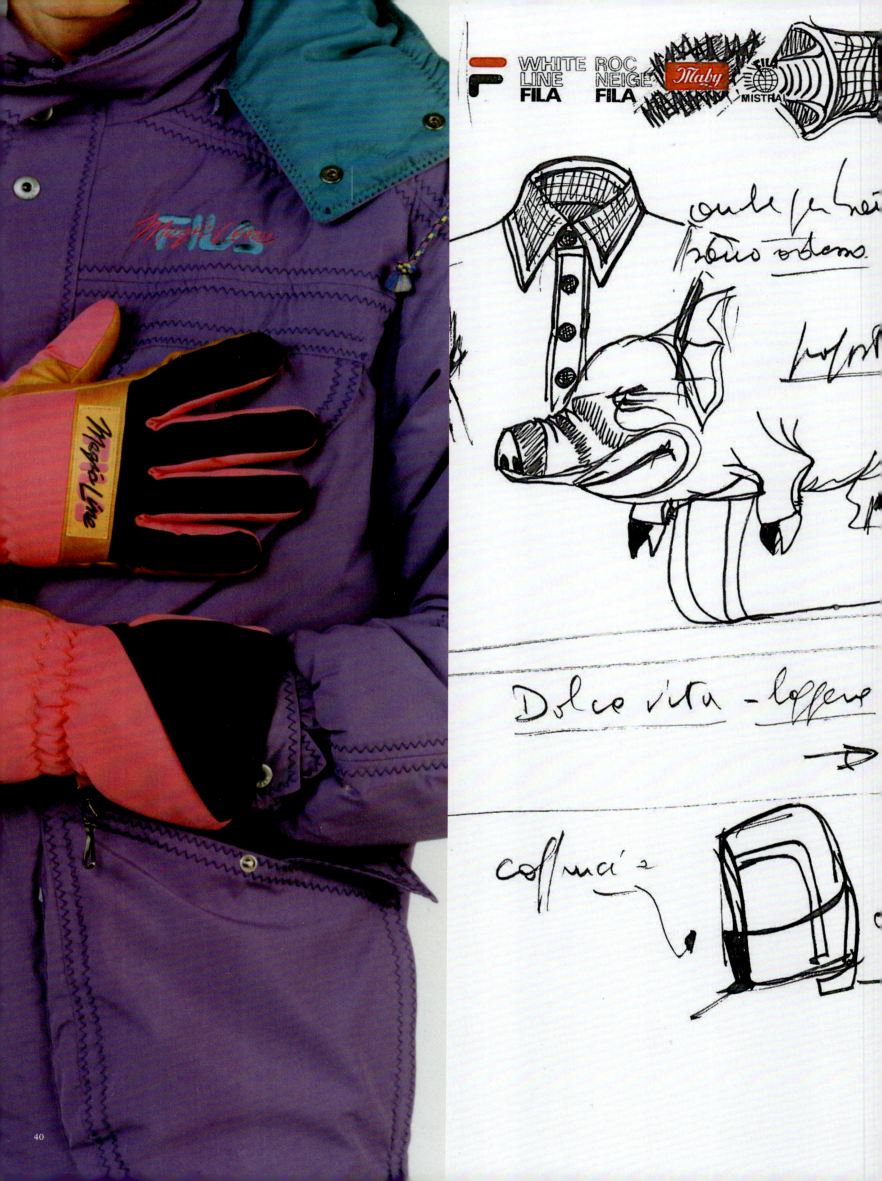

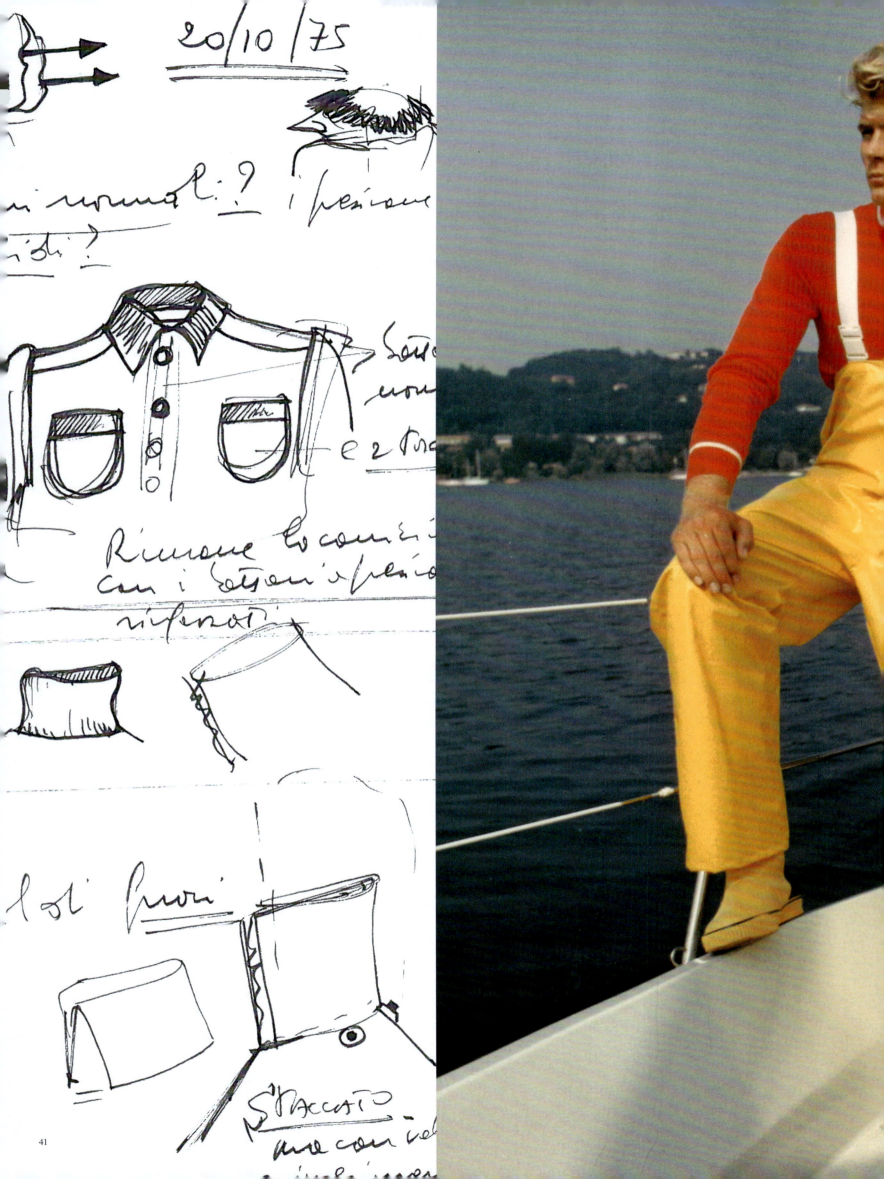

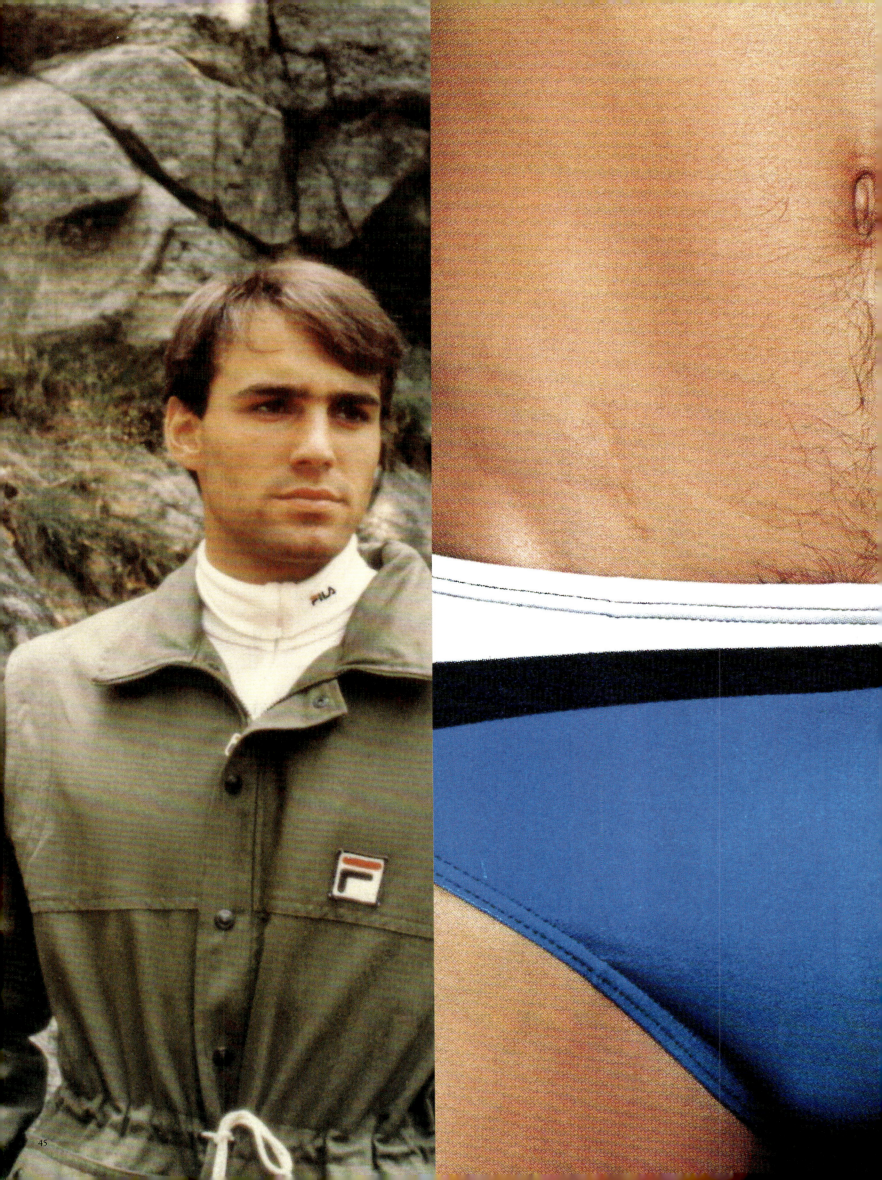

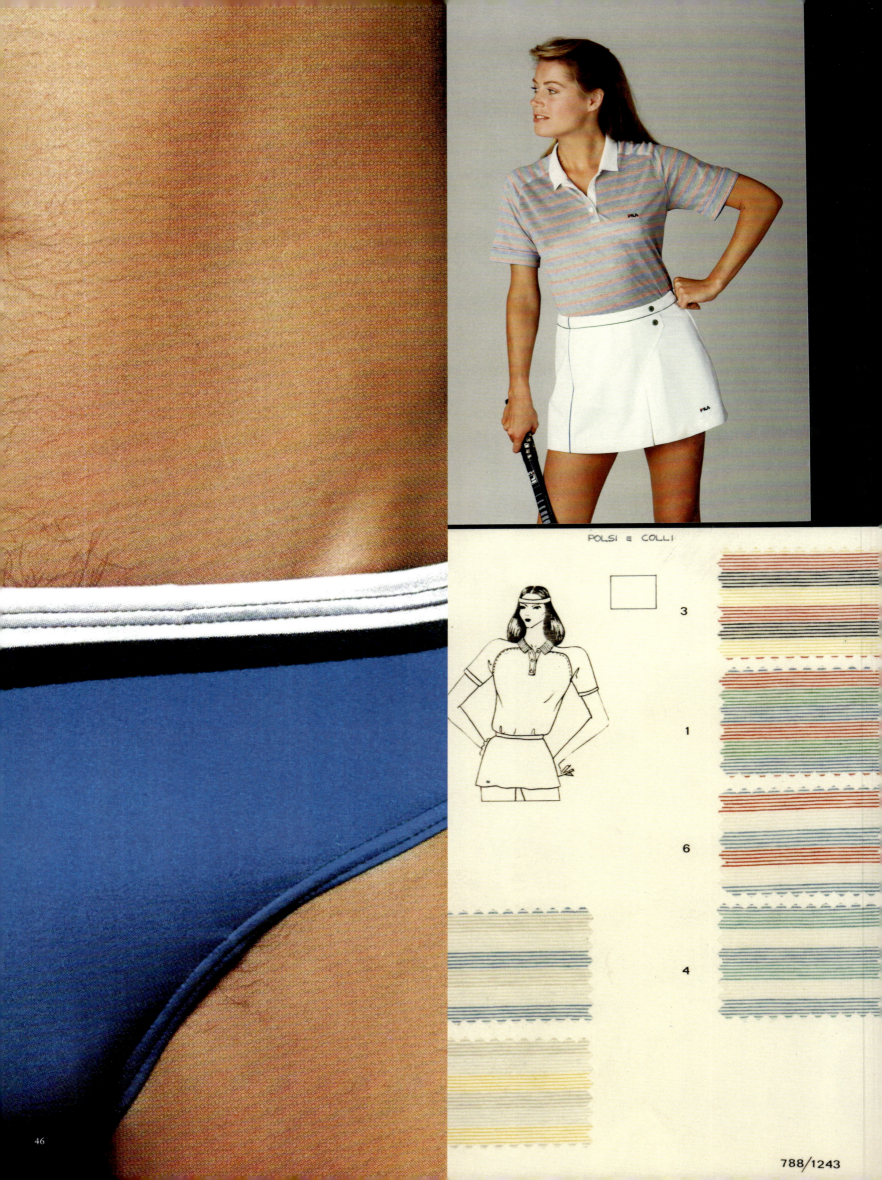

EVERYTHING FALLS
Silvia Calderoni

Phlebas the Phoenician, a fortnight dead,
Forgot the cry of gulls, and the deep seas swell
And the profit and loss:
A current under sea
Picked his bones in whispers. As he rose and fell
He passed the stages of his age and youth
Entering the whirlpool.
Gentile or Jew
O you who turn the wheel and look to windward,
Consider Phlebas, who was once handsome and tall as you.
(T. S. Eliot, *The Waste Land*, Part IV – Death by Water)

My body is warm and my name is Greg. Smooth flesh, polished day after day by the ocean currents and the chemistry of the chlorine. Someone who loved me very much one night whispered in my ear that I was the one who altered the course of the evolution lines, creating a bridge between the sky and the sea and between a human being and a fish. A new species that descends from *Homo sapiens* but that abandons its destructive features. He told me amid the vapors of our bodies that the new name was *Homo sentiens*, the man who feels, the man with feelings. I knew he was inventing every word, perhaps he was a writer and a lover of science fiction, I had imagined it because he kept on his night table, along with some used tissues and a jar of vaseline, some scattered sheets written in ballpoint pen and a paperback edition of Huxley's *Brave New World*. I can't remember his voice now, but his aftershave smelled like jasmine and his right hand was always stained blue like the ocean. Then, that same night, at the first signs of dawn, I had one of my usual crises and I got out of bed. I put on a pair of underpants that were tight around my genitals still stained by the color of the sea and close to the edge of the tub I opened my arms so they were parallel to the horizon line. And I leaped and took flight. I slipped away without leaving even a single scale in between the sheets. Not even a feather at the foot of the bed.

My body is trained and my name is Greg. I have always believed I was born from an egg. Like birds or fish or turtles. My mother and father got me when I had already been made and shaped, and that time I spent in the shell comes to mind only when on the bottom of the pool the bubbles that come out of my nose clash with my eyeballs. From when I was a child I trained my organs, nerves, and capillaries to listen, wait, to build up speeches, to answer questions and to argue every point. I didn't like going to school, sitting there surrounded by misbehaved children who more often than not would look at me askance. Nor did I like to accumulate notions and burden my head, which was light and always brought me back to the surface of the water quickly. In spite of this, every morning, hidden in my room, my ligaments would hold long sessions of trigonometry, quantum physics, philosophy, and poetry. Bundles of nerves that recited by heart the hendecasyllables of Dante, of Petrarch, and of all the kings of unrequited love. I kept as a secret from all those around me Shakespeare's sonnets and Blake's poetry, and day after day my mother looked at me the way you would a puzzle. Each afternoon, after diving practice, I would lock myself inside the kitchen pantry, turn on the light, and sit on the crate of water bottles as I watched my cartilage practice calligraphy: elegant, ornate writing, capital letters, with those large curves of blue ink that folded back onto themselves to then slide into sophisticated double consonants, identical to one another, without trembling, without splashing, without smudging. And among those jars of green olives that our grandparents would ship to us from Greece, I learned the secret of the twists and would transform the italics into pike dives. At night, before falling asleep, I liked to listen to the muscles of my legs read me the book of Greek myths along with Medusa, Calypso, Stheno, and Euryale, mythological creatures related to the oceans. I had borrowed their names to rename each diving board at the pool where I practiced. But the most exciting story of all was the one about Icarus and his mad flight into the sun. When my quadriceps, my adductors, and my calves read this story to me, all of them together, I could see them swell and grow strong and symmetrical, ready to uphold, should they appear, two pairs of wings in my heels.

My body is elegant and my name is Greg. At dance school I heard Johann Sebastian Bach's *Prelude in C Major* for the first time. A young man with tapered fingers played it on the piano for us young ballet dancers at the barre. We trained doing pliés, développés, grands ronds de jambe, and pirouettes: each figure had a form to adhere to, while my back stretched upward like one of the thousands of Yucca trees in the Joshua Tree desert. Since then that sound has been like constant background music in my ears, wedged inside my auricles, in the daith pits, and can't get out. A perpetual tinnitus of piano sonatas, one of those secrets I have never told anyone. I saw the boy who was playing many years later, he was applauding me from an arena filled with people. His hands were more those of an adult now, but the elegant way he sat had drawn my attention, opening up a gap in my memory while I rotated my neck at the edge of the pool. Once more I felt the taste of the salty skin of his cheeks during that first mistaken kiss behind the piano. I smile to think of the instant both of us closed our eyes, hesitantly coming closer, missing each other's mouths and candidly kissing each other's cheeks. That day I won the platform competition while his hands played Bach in my ears.

My body is luminous and my name is Greg. When I was an adolescent, each day I would sharpen my bones like pencil tips. So many times I found them at the poolside bending one against the other and drawing triangles and parallel lines on the surface, exposing and demonstrating to the bones of other adolescents at the peak of puberty the Euclidean theorems, Archimedes' levers, and Galileo's discoveries concerning the way objects fall and their acceleration. Bones whitened by the chlorine and tanned by the sun. Heats, lists, teams, piles. My skeleton had already started winning, but the more I won the more my eyes saw the clear pool water being transformed into black puddles and every diving board into a cliff. Until the national championships, when my hesitation was so evident my mother rushed to the edge of the pool to interrupt the race. She grabbed me by the arm and took me away, at first out of the pool, then out of the parking lot, and then away from everything, to a place where there was just her and me. She looked me straight in the eye and told me that whatever I did, whatever music I listened to, whoever's body I kissed, whatever cloud passed me by, whatever disease invaded my body, she would always and in any case be beside me. I went back in and won the race hands down.

My body is wild and my name is Greg. In summertime, during summer vacations, I would climb the white mountains on the Nevada border. I would take my feet to these heights, to train on the ravines, allowing them to catch their breath after a whole season of holding up the weight of all that I am. I would climb all the way up to the juniper scrub and take my shoes and socks off, letting my almost webbed toes stare at the dizzying overhangs surrounding me. From that bighorn-sheep ridge I watched the eagles take flight from the mountain crests. I studied the peace they felt the instant before they pushed off, that ambiguous time when not doing becomes doing as if it were a miracle, a calling from another planet. I watched them spread their wings in their majesty, and when I closed my eyes I felt my toenails digging into the earth like sharp talons. Then, when my senses were inebriated, I would climb down as far as the Owens Valley searching for sandy soil in which to plunge my stiff arms. I entered the ground with both limbs parallel, without raising a single grain of dust as I searched for the roots of the plants. I liked to stroke them, and they, timidly, exchanged my affection, telling the palms of my hands about how they held on in spite of the strong winds, the storms, the cheers of the crowds filling the stadiums.

My body is alone and my name is Greg. We had decided to meet on the Malibu wharf at around six thirty before the sun went down. As I walked toward him I watched him stare at the ocean, a sports bag over his shoulder. I immediately noticed his skin burnt from the sun on the beach, I could see it through the undershirt he was wearing. The sleeves were so loose I enjoyed the silhouette of his tiny nipples. His wavy hair covered a part of his face and came down to his shoulders. I can't remember his voice. For a long time we embraced, watching the cormorants dive straight into the water, like arrows shot by the gods, and then re-emerge quickly as if they were revenants on their way back from the kingdom of the dead. Each time, to be able to stay with him, I had to fill my lungs and hold my breath, he was so different from me that I could immerse myself in his world, but I could not drink a single drop of its water. And then I gasped for breath and I resurfaced leaving some of my sadness with him.

My body is ready and my name is Greg. I was too young when I began competing with the elements, challenging the logic of the above and the below, slicing the air while challenging the force of gravity. Already as a child I was a star in that leap before diving. I arrived at my first Olympics so sure of myself I knew my name would be among those of the poets in my school book. My category was that of the ten-meter platform, also known as that of the short poems. So much had I trained that I had even learned to leave my agitation far from the diving board, in the pockets of my bathrobe, together with my plastic slippers. My trainer and I had prepared an exercise that was simple but clean, devoid of rhymes or rhetorical figures that risked weighing it down. I had prepared *The Waste Land* by T. S. Eliot, a classic, so great a classic that if I had executed it poorly, I would no doubt have received a very low score. And instead I get up on the platform with my hair still wet from the dive for the qualifiers, I walk to the edge, I fill my lungs with air, I hold my arms out parallel to the horizon, I close my eyes and enter that secret. Then, I explode. The words, the figures, come out one after another, linked together like pearls in a necklace. The leap time is short, it is a time during which I suspend everything and the skeleton holds the rhythm given by the punctuation. And as I leap, I feel the sun, the scent of jasmine, and I manage to end the last verse with a period. A precise period, made with blue ink. With no splashes. With no smudges.

My body is the last one and my name is Greg.

951/3233/8

951/3233/1

951/3233/10

951/3233/11

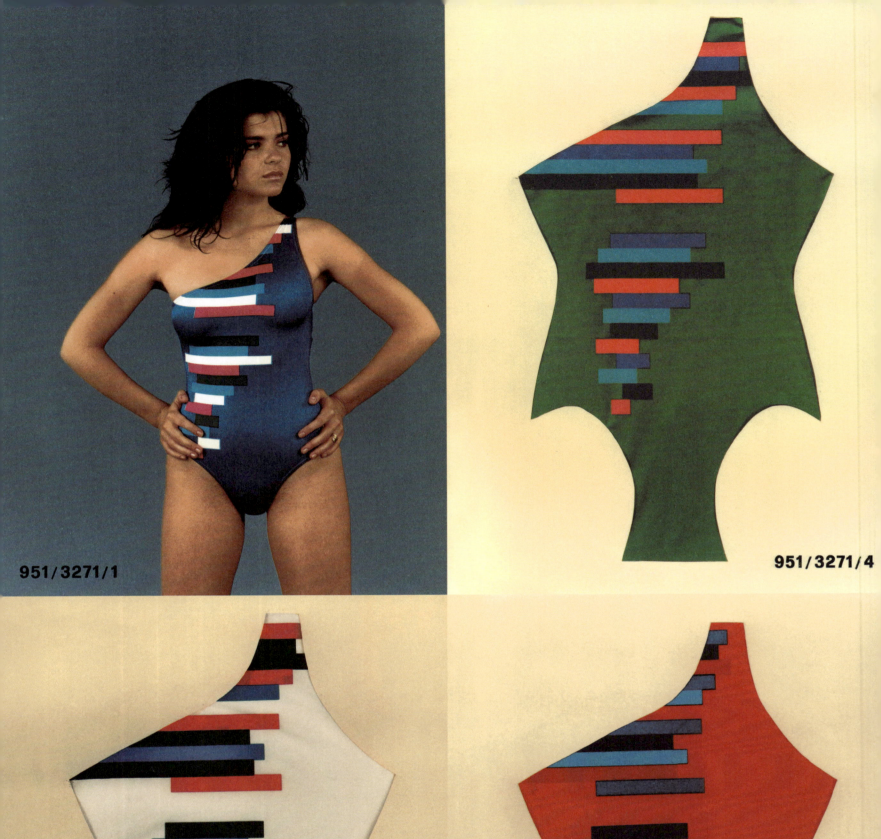

951/3271/1

951/3271/4

951/3271/3

951/3271/2

951/3275/5

951/3275/2

951/3275/1

951/3275/3

951/3292/3

951/3292/4

951/3292/6

951/3292/1

936/3445/1

936/3445/2

936/3445/4

936/3445/5

936/3445/3

THE THIN RED LINES
Matteo Codignola

As in every self-respecting museum, the FILA Museum in Biella exhibits a number of very interesting pieces, plus one that alone is well worth making the trip—and that I almost missed. We had already visited several rooms dedicated to other sports, and when we got to the tennis room, I immediately focused on the pictures of the FILA kids on the walls, in search of a story to tell.

Which is no easy task. Talking about Panatta & Bertolucci after *Una squadra* would be like explaining Gassman and Trintignant to someone who has already seen *Il sorpasso*, while everything that can be said about a giant, now wounded, like Guillermo Vilas, has been said, for better or, at least once, very authoritatively, even for worse: "Vilas writes poems the way I play tennis" (Jorge Luis Borges).

So? So, luckily we had the women, who, those who follow tennis—as well as the organizers of major tournaments, and their audiences—generally tend to snub, often losing out on the best in terms of drama, comedy, plus a series of intermediate nuances, and not just on the court. All it took was one look at the ladies before me and I knew that with them it would only be a question of what, or who, needed to be sacrificed. Andrea Jaeger. Today no one remembers who she was, but if she hadn't been seriously injured right after her debut she would probably have become one of the greatest stars of the 1980s. And instead, first she earned a degree in Theology, then she prepared to take Holy Orders, which at a certain point she actually did. Gabriela Sabatini. In the very limited number of those who have a right to the status of diva, and not only as concerns tennis, Gabriela obviously followed Lenglen (who invented it): but long before Sharapova, so to speak. Pam Shriver. Well, if someone wants to get an idea of just how crazy, excessive, rickety—and fun—professional tennis was in the 1980s, all they need to do is listen, on the radio or on a podcast, to any one of her irresistible stories. And then—off to one side, as is fitting—there was my favorite. Wearing an emerald green outfit, Evonne Goolagong would stretch way out on the grass to be able to hit a very low backhand, which I was sure she had turned into a win. This often happened to her, against her colleagues whom she managed to beat every other game— players like Chris Evert, Billie Jean King, or Martina Navrátilová. Today they're the ones we talk about the most—or maybe they're the ones doing the talking, also because they did, after all, invent modern women's tennis. In any case, during those same years Evonne won, without beating around the bush, seven Grand Slams. This Wiradjuri Aborigine was as lethal and impeccable on the court as she was radiant off it, where when asked to she was happy to entertain friends and admirers —Liza Minnelli and Andy Warhol, among others—on the meaning of her last name ("kangaroo nose"), the strange place where she'd grown up (her parents' trailer parked in the middle of the bush), or the even stranger place where she had learned to play (a court covered in red sand created inside a wrecking yard). Yes, I was just thinking that there would be a lot to say about Evonne. Except that, at that very same moment, Daniele, the young museum curator who was showing me around, asked me if I wanted to see something.

In any other exhibition space that *something* would at least have been reproduced on a poster outside and lit up with a suitable number of spotlights. But this was Piedmont, and they had simply placed the object in a small glass display case in the middle of the room. It was a polo shirt that had at one time been white, but was now rather yellowed. In homage to the mysterious physical law that shrinks pieces of clothing before the species for which they were designed expands, it also seemed tiny. But no matter. What was important, really important, were the thin vertical lines that one day in 1972 Pierluigi Rolando, FILA's designer at the time, tried to draw on it with a red pencil, and that, albeit somewhat faded, are still there. Seen that way, this sartorial sketch presented itself as what it probably was, the risk one starts out from when one seeks something completely new. At the time Rolando was imagining the company's first tennis line; in fact, he had decided to ignore the company's long and austere history, opting for a tribute—think of it—to baseball, and in particular to the shirt worn by its brightest star, Babe Ruth. Now. No one knows whether Rolando and the managers at FILA who later approved the sketch realized it entirely, but placing another sport—and a *popular* one at that—next to a game that had grown in the cult of its own uniqueness risked being seen, by the world of tennis, as a scandal. And the best was yet to come. Those red lines—combined with the showy red and blue "F" stitched onto the chest, which made crocodiles, kangaroos, and laurel wreaths look like relics from a past that was suddenly almost exotic—were in fact an explicit and irreverent challenge to the establishment of tennis, to its fortresses (Wimbledon, to name just one), and, above all, to the element that players, spectators, and lovers of the sport had always attributed an almost religious reverence to: the color white.

An element that apparently no one was—nor had ever been—willing to barter. Although it had happened almost by chance—in Victorian England the game had spread so quickly that the first tennis players, not knowing what to put on, presented themselves on the court dressed for cricket—the color white had almost immediately become *de rigueur*, and just as immediately an identifying feature of the new sport as such, and of all that it had quickly ended up signifying in territories of style as well as customs. Consequently, there were no exceptions, except for colored stripes on socks or on the V-neck and the cuffs of sweaters. Years later Wimbledon would even put in writing the color that every proper tennis player should wear: *predominantly white*.

Even if, in everyday practice, there's white and then there's *white*. Our federal masters, in the 1960s, for instance, almost all wore a shade that for us layfolk was inaccessible. In their case, shorts, shirts, and socks—often still made of wool—were all in various cream tones, which was sometimes intense, and seemed to come from that unchangeable and remote antiquity in which tennis, who knows why, loves to imagine itself. No one really even knew where they got them, seeing that in the stores where our mothers shopped the clothes that were available were also a rather normal optical white. In any case, the difference in color was clear to see and I suspect we weren't the only ones to have noticed it. Perhaps there was an opening there, the people at FILA must have thought. And so, one fine day in the early 1970s, the best players in the tennis clubs—the ones who in a certain sense obviously played wearing the right outfits, rather than grabbing things from the laundry basket the way we did—switched the symbol of their rank, abandoning their Lacostes in favor of an outfit that reminded them of the one worn by their coaches. With one small, yet rather significant, difference in nuance: those shirts and shorts were unquestionably beige (and their collars unquestionably blue). Which led to the umpteenth almost Talmudic discussion, the same as the endless ones on which that sport invented by gentlemen, hence based on few clear rules and a number of implicit prohibitions, had nourished itself from the beginning: in short, were those *somethings* still white, or weren't they? So could they, or could they not, be worn? And those new shirts, was it my impression alone, weren't they sort of light blue? And if they were, my goodness, where would it end?

Impassioned debates that, believe it or not, continued for months. And they would probably have heated up, like many other equally futile ones, if they hadn't been superseded, from one day to the next, thanks to the second appearance at Wimbledon of Björn Borg.

Not that his first, in 1973, had gone unnoticed. Today it is hard to get an idea of what "Borgasm" was like, but already at his debut at the All England Club, Borg had, without wanting to, provoked the sudden reappearance of a malady that on the island was thought to have been extinct for years—Beatlemania. Rushed at the club entrance by some three hundred girls who had lost control of themselves, and poorly defended by some police who were totally unprepared, the Teen Angel (or Viking God, depending on the tabloid) had been overwhelmed, escaping with some difficulty and a tiny bit scared from the mob. The undignified melee repeated itself for the whole time that Borg was scheduled to play, causing more than one eyebrow to be raised by the ladies and gentlemen of the Centre Court, and the tabloids mentioned above to open many a bottle of champagne. To the extent that the following year, in the weeks prior to the tournament, the police sent a circular letter to the principals of the schools in the area asking them to nip any madness in the bud, eventually restricting it to the classroom, and under lock and key at that.

Borg had thus been able to train in peace, and at the right moment present himself on the tennis court wearing a red uniform. With underneath it, Rolando's red-striped polo shirt. Now it was clear who it had been designed for.

It's hard to say whether FILA's first investment at the time was a stroke of genius, of luck, or, as in the best of cases, a combination of the two. No doubt someone in Biella, in 1972 or 1973, had figured out that the young man, whom everyone was talking about practically without ever having seen him play, would soon become not only a tennis superstar, but the best endorsement ever. Borg was indeed very different from his colleagues, from every point of view. To begin with, he hardly spoke. When asked what the secrets of his game were, he would answer: always send the ball to the other side. And as for the idolatry he was the object of, he looked at it from afar—to be exact, from the inside of the hotel rooms where he lived with his coach and adoptive father, Lennart Bergelin, at such low temperatures that during the night the strings on the rackets would break, just like icebergs in the Arctic darkness. On the other hand, he could beat practically anyone, with a kind of tennis that before his time simply did not exist, and that no one could as yet even understand. Ah, and all this, thanks to his ascertained resistance to taking off his playing clothes, dressed in FILA from his head to his toes. If he hadn't existed, some advertiser would have had to invent him. Or maybe Wes Anderson would have, come to think of it.

Whatever the case may be, in the space of a few seasons the Angelic Assassin, which is how Borg was finally dubbed, and especially the other esteemed members of the merry men—McEnroe, Connors, Năstase, Gerulaitis—would wipe out the tennis they had been born into, proving how hiding behind those white gestures was actually a (very) dark side: theirs. Of that fire that lasted years FILA had no doubt lit a spark, but with a revolution that was all its own, made of velvet—or of pastel. And over time it remained loyal to those thin red lines, dressing players who did not necessarily win Grand Slams, but who beyond a shadow of a doubt *were* tennis. Like whom? Like John Isner, to name just one. In 2010, on Court 18 at Wimbledon, Isner played (and won) against Nicolas Mahut the longest match in history, which ended after more than eleven hours in three days, scoring 70–68 in the fifth set. Because of the characteristics of the two players, it was an anomalous game, and on the fifth seemingly never-ending set, one of the craziest ever seen. Isner would serve and earn his four points, almost always to love. Then Mahut would serve and earn his, also to love. And then on and on and on. It seemed like it would never end. Sometimes, seeing Isner today, you get the idea that for him it still isn't over: that he's actually still playing, and precisely so that it will never end. But this is not a hallucination, neither his nor our own.

Simply put, it's tennis.

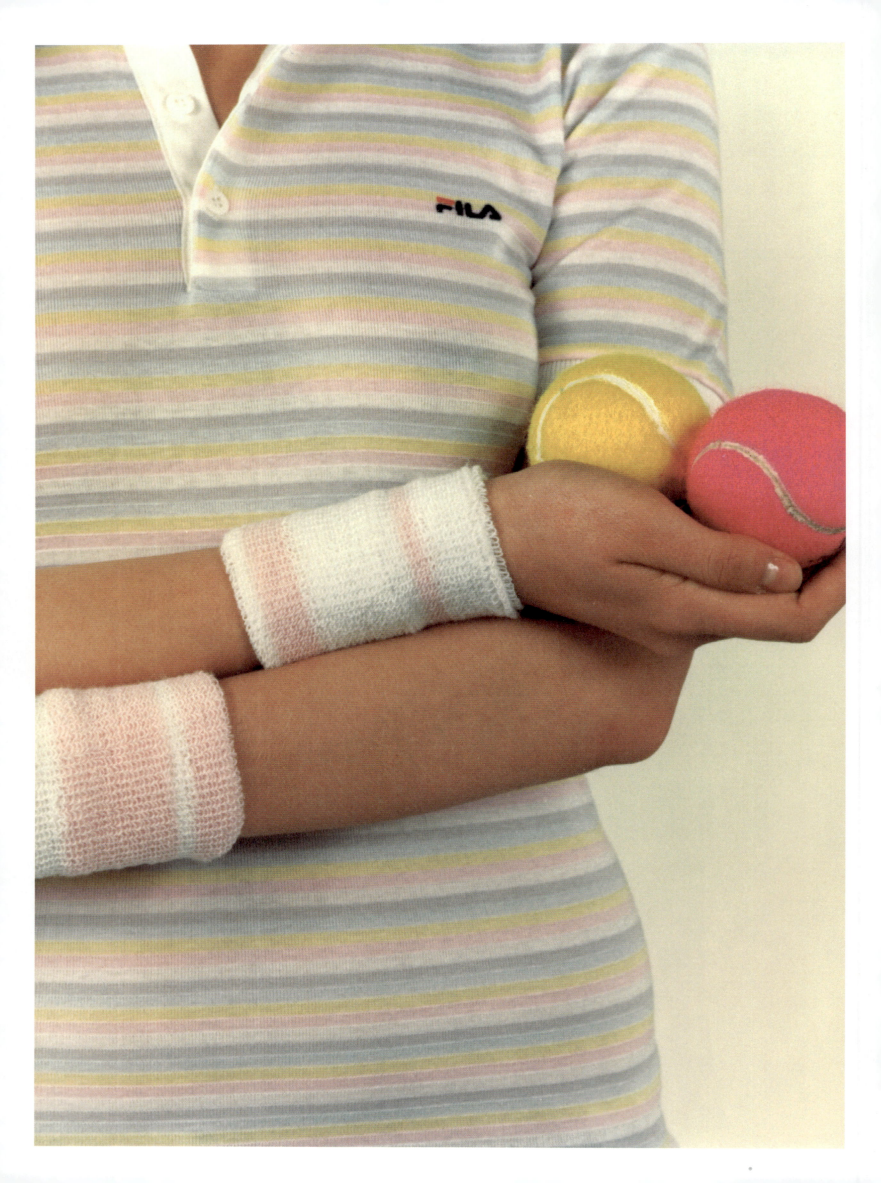

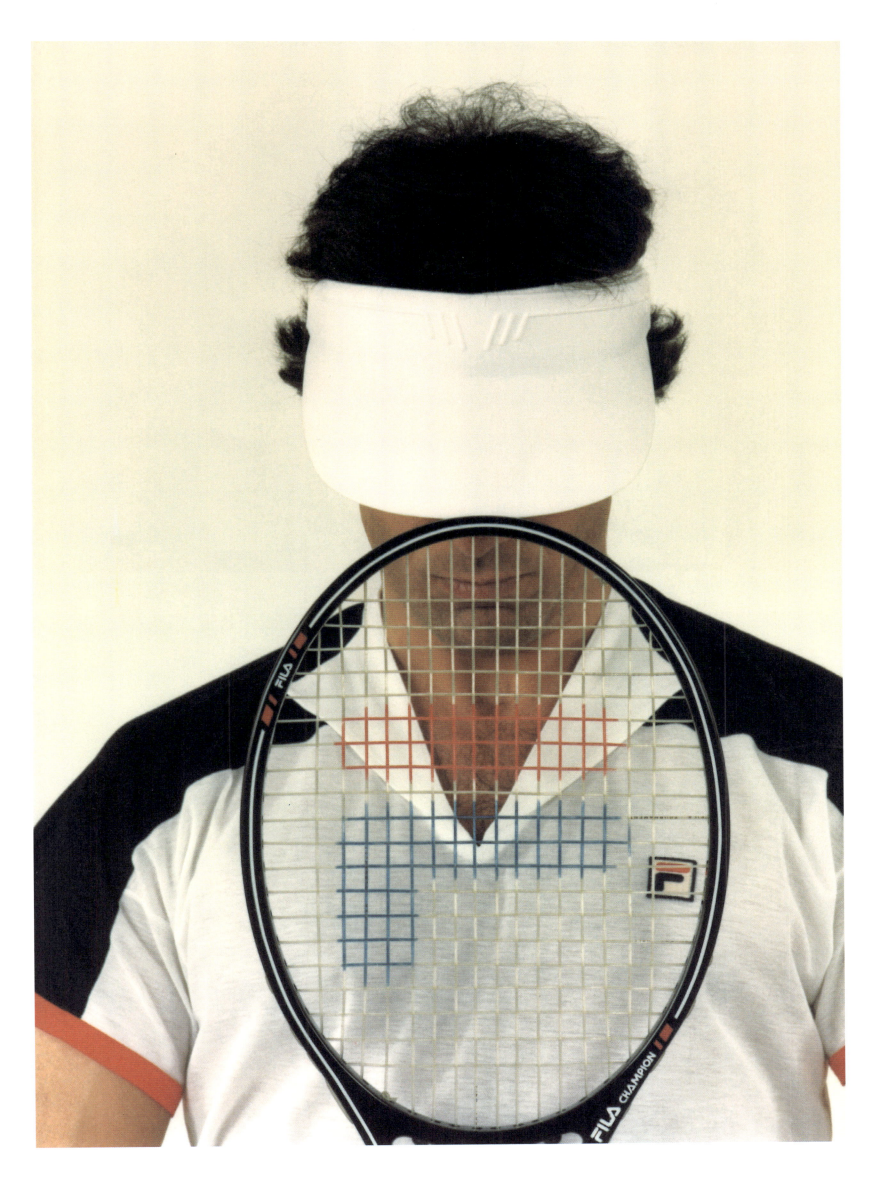

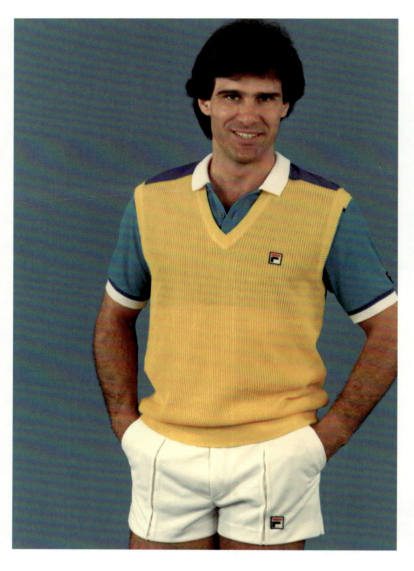

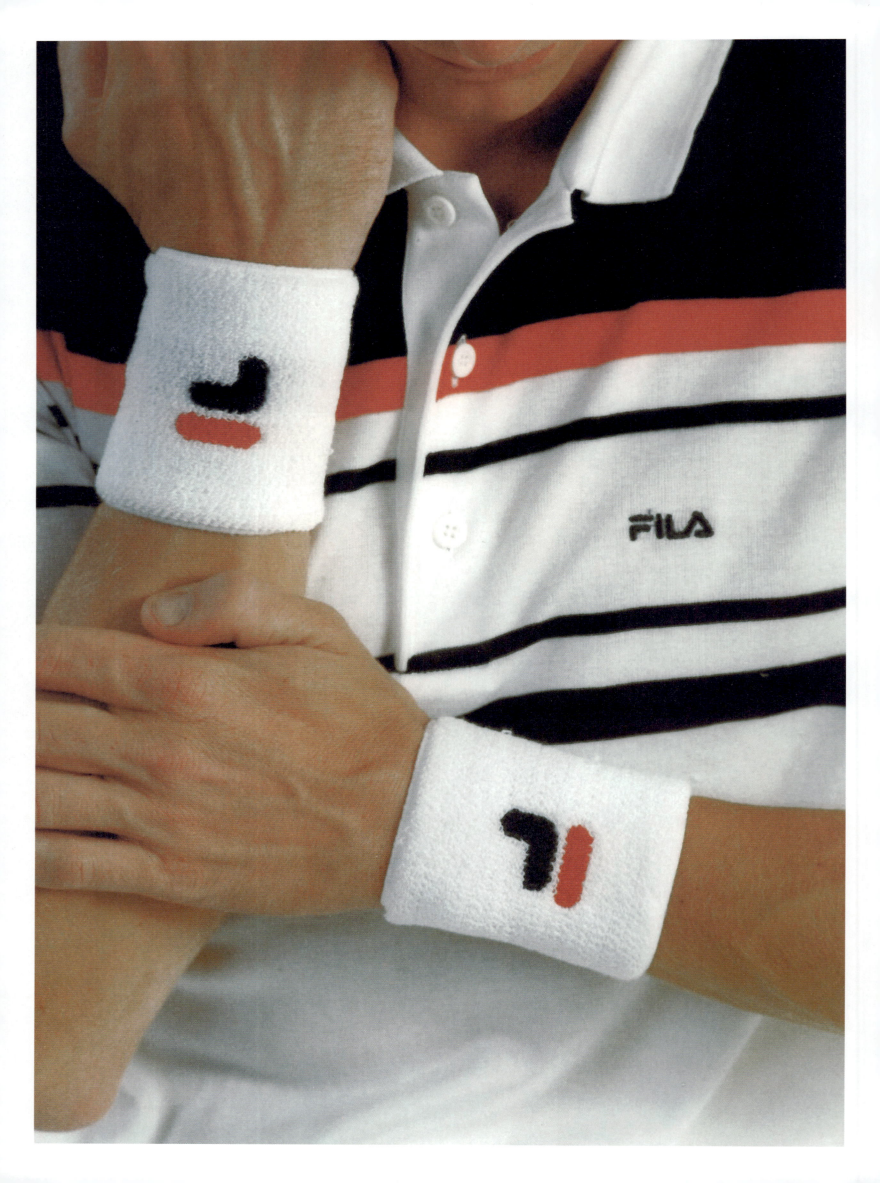

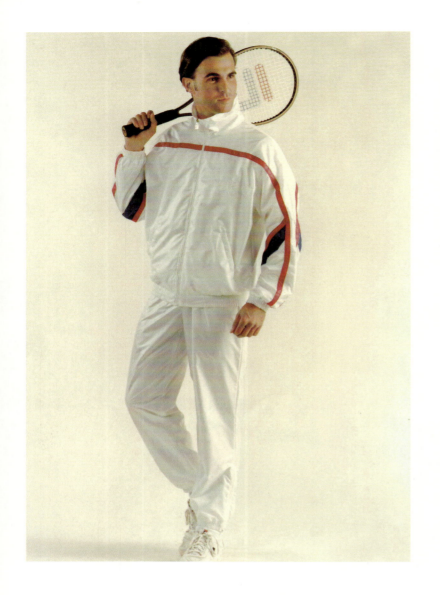

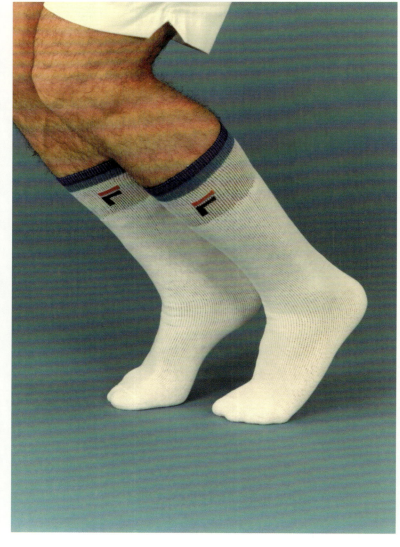
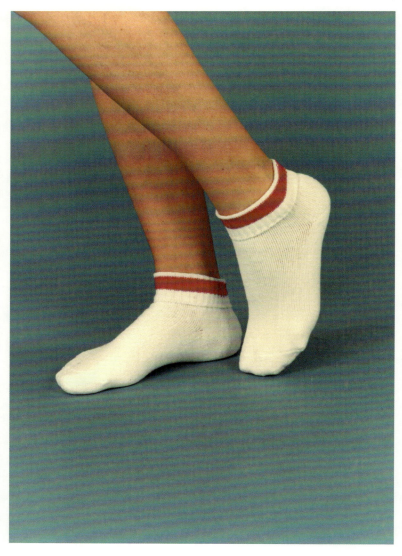

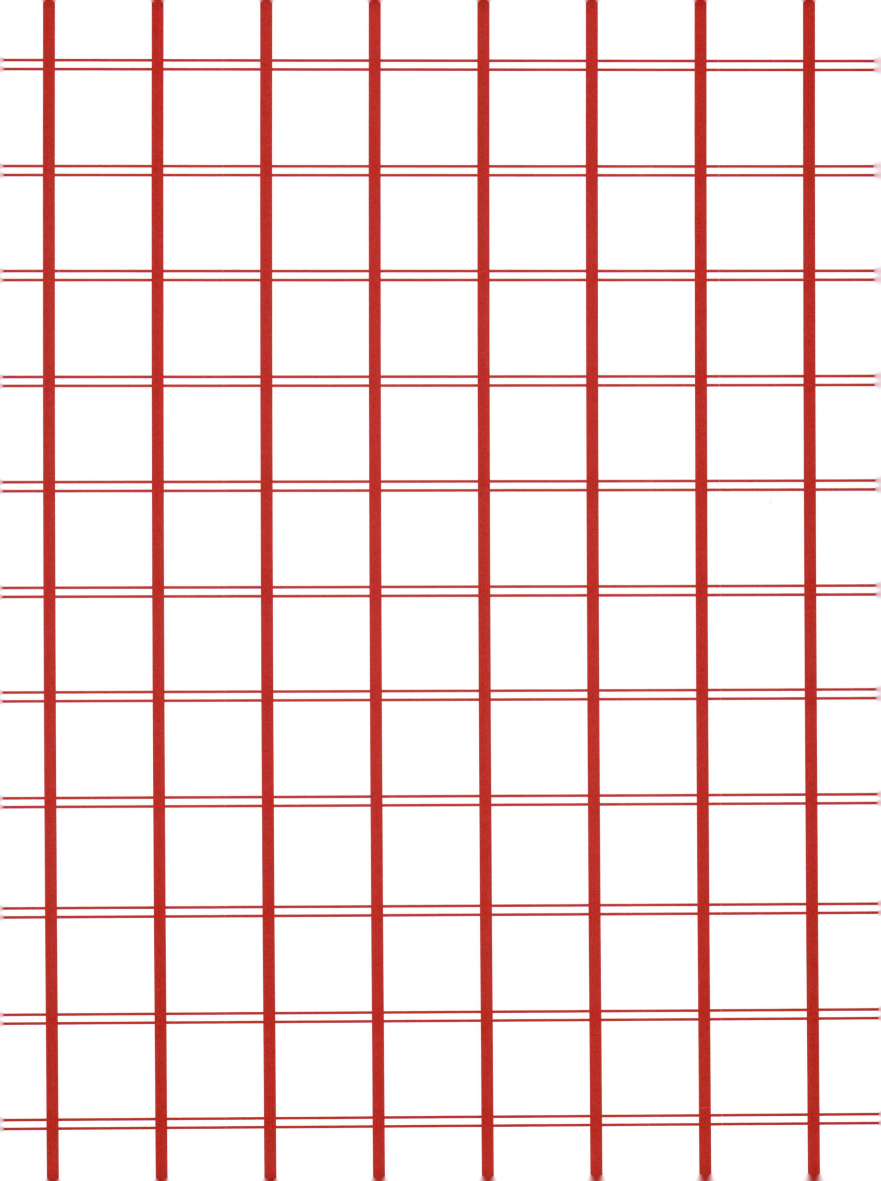

Björn Borg on TV Fifteen LOVE Lucky Stripes Lucky Strikes Thirty LOOOVE Forty LOOOOOOOOOVE Smash Strike SCORE FILA Family FILA Guy FILA

Future Björn Borg Björn Borg on TV Fifteen LOVE Lucky Stripes Lucky Strikes Thirty LOOOVE Forty LOOOOOOOOOVE Smash Strike SCORE FILA

Family FILA Guy FILA Future Björn Borg Björn Borg on TV Fifteen LOVE Lucky Stripes Lucky Strikes Thirty LOOOVE Forty LOOOOO

Strike SCORE FILA Family FILA Guy FILA Future Björn Borg Björn Borg on TV Fifteen LOVE Lucky Stripes Lucky Strikes Thirty LOO

OOOOOOVE Smash Strike SCORE FILA Family FILA Guy FILA Future Björn Borg Björn Borg on TV Fifteen LOVE Lucky Stripes Lucky

OVE Forty LOOOOOOOOOVE Smash Strike SCORE FILA Family FILA Guy FILA Future Björn Borg Björn Borg on TV Fifteen LOVE

Strikes Thirty LOOOVE Forty LOOOOOOOOOVE Smash Strike SCORE FILA Family FILA Guy FILA Future Björn Borg Björn Borg

Lucky Stripes Lucky Strikes Thirty LOOOVE Forty LOOOOOOOOOVE Smash Strike SCORE FILA Family FILA Guy FILA Future

on TV Fifteen LOVE Lucky Stripes Lucky Strikes Thirty LOOOVE Forty LOOOOOOOOOVE Smash Strike SCORE FILA Family

Björn Borg Björn Borg on TV Fifteen LOVE Lucky Stripes Lucky Strikes Thirty LOOOVE Forty LOOOOOOOOOVE Smash Strike

FILA Guy FILA Future Björn Borg Björn Borg on TV Fifteen LOVE Lucky Stripes Lucky Strikes Thirty LOOOVE Forty LOOOOOOOOO

SCORE FILA Family FILA Guy FILA Future Björn Borg Björn Borg on TV Fifteen LOVE Lucky Stripes Lucky Strikes Thirty LOOOVE Forty LOOOOOOOO

BJÖRN BORG'S POLO – Karl Holmqvist

Short Shorts and Fast Balls BB BB BB BB BB BB BB BB BB BB BB BB BB BB BB BB BB BB BB BB on TV Smash Strike SCORE FILA Family FILA Guy FILA Future Short Shorts and

Fast Balls BB BB BB BB BB BB BB BB BB BB BB BB BB BB BB BB BB BB BB BB on TV Smash Strike SCORE FILA Family FILA Guy FILA Future Short Shorts and Fast Balls

BB BB BB BB BB BB BB BB BB BB BB BB BB BB BB BB BB BB BB BB on TV Smash Strike SCORE FILA Family FILA Guy FILA Future Short Shorts and Fast Balls BB BB

BB BB BB BB BB BB BB BB BB BB BB BB BB BB BB BB BB BB on TV Smash Strike SCORE FILA Family FILA Guy FILA Future Short Shorts and Fast Balls BB BB BB BB

on TV Smash Strike SCORE FILA Family FILA Guy FILA Future Short Shorts and Fast Balls BB BB BB BB BB BB BB BB BB BB BB BB BB BB BB BB BB BB BB BB on TV Smash Strike

SCORE FILA Family FILA Guy FILA Future Short Shorts and Fast Balls BB BB BB BB BB BB BB BB BB BB BB BB BB BB BB BB BB BB BB BB on TV Smash Strike SCORE

FILA Guy FILA Future Short Shorts and Fast Balls BB BB BB BB BB BB BB BB BB BB BB BB BB BB BB BB BB BB BB BB on TV Smash Strike SCORE FILA Family FILA Future

Short Shorts and Fast Balls BB BB BB BB BB BB BB BB BB BB BB BB BB BB BB BB BB BB BB BB on TV Smash Strike SCORE FILA Family FILA Guy FILA Future Short Shorts and

Fast Balls BB BB BB BB BB BB BB BB BB BB BB BB BB BB BB BB BB BB BB BB on TV Smash Strike SCORE FILA Family FILA Guy FILA Future Short Shorts and Fast Balls

BB BB BB BB BB BB BB BB BB BB BB BB BB BB BB BB BB BB BB BB on TV Smash Strike SCORE FILA Family FILA Guy FILA Future Short Shorts and Fast Balls BB BB

BB BB BB BB BB BB BB BB BB BB BB BB BB BB BB BB BB BB on TV Smash Strike SCORE FILA Family FILA Guy FILA Future Short Shorts and Fast Balls BB BB BB BB

on TV Smash Strike SCORE FILA Family FILA Guy FILA Future Short Shorts and Fast Balls BB BB BB BB BB BB BB BB BB BB BB BB BB BB BB BB BB BB BB BB on TV Smash Strike

MEMORY TEST – ATHLETES AND AMBASSADORS
Carlo Antonelli

Borges once wrote: "We are our memory, we are that chimerical museum of shifting shapes," (*Funes the Memorious*, 1942). My recollection of the FILA brand is linked to the metal snaps on a fantastic polo shirt with blue trim everywhere, and a red collar, that I would button and unbutton constantly when I was 12 years old. I had never played tennis. And yet I did own a pair of those white shorts with "that" magical square at the bottom of one side. I lived in a sort of "Garden of the Finzi-Continis," but with disco music. My family came from the Piedmont Valley, and had rented a large area with fields and woods to a dynasty of Genoese oil tycoons who had moved to my great-grandparents' village for fear of being kidnapped (there were bodyguards everywhere lurking around with walkie-talkies). They had built a marvelous swimming pool that they invited all the local kids to come swim in. There was also a big warehouse/dressing area with a bar that made sodas, and a fabulous hi-fi system with a mixer and two Technics turntables on which we played LPs by Cerrone, Barry White & The Love Unlimited Orchestra, Gloria Gaynor, of course Donna Summer, and the solo album by Giorgio Moroder—in other words, disco. They had also built a perfect, professional tennis court, surrounded by mountain firs, ten minutes on foot from the residential area. There we would go, I would go, to see the matches and the tournaments. The FILA brand was everywhere. Behind the clay courts was the crazy, immense hunting reserve located on what had at one time been my grandparents' land, repopulated with doe and deer that would eventually shed their horns all over the place.

In any case, I was crazy about tennis on TV, about the elegance, Adriano Panatta's and Guillermo Vilas's fabulous pre-Dyson-styled forelocks, about Paolo Bertolucci, about that season. FILA—in that space and time—was everywhere. Televised tennis was endless, interrupted every now and again by the grunts and groans produced by the muscular strain and by the sound of the ball—beautiful—as well as by the discreet utterances made by the umpire keeping the score. The temporal exaggeration of some very important matches, the strange geometry of the doubles… It was one of the few sports about which I knew everything. And I was really into the shirts and the shorts (picture Boris Becker at his peak), and above all pleated skirts, which reminded me of the Japanese anime that private Italian TV networks—the only ones in the world—were chock-full of. But another parallel and mysterious world was that of the Olympics watched during those summers filled with tedium — at the most absurd times of the day because of the crazy time differences—capable of generating rare forms of hypnosis (suffice it to recall the great marathons, which had also always been a colonial triumph, with the Kenyan athletes wearing lightweight FILA outfits: Tergat, Tanui, Lagat, Okayo). We also watched the Winter Olympics games on Rai 1, broadcast from mysterious North American locations (picture Alberto Tomba, massive inside what looked more like a combat uniform). Back then (what is now referred to as "gorpcore"), I already loved sports stores, technical sportswear especially for the mountains (Reinhold Messner comes to mind, donning his mountain headgear, 1977, and before him the mountain climber Giorgio Bertone, 1975). Inside these marvelous commercial caverns were posters with ambassadors for FILA, and not just as concerned tennis. Although what stood out on the middle wall, behind the cash register, was the one with Björn Borg, "FILA for Champions." *Boom*.

These are my memories, and I hope I haven't recalled them incorrectly.

Yes, because according to the most recent studies in neuroscience, the exact same brain network is activated whether a person is remembering the past or imagining the future. This is "one of the adaptive functions of memory: it allows us to plan for the future. It provides the building blocks for mental time travel" (Cody Kommers, "Faulty Memory Is a Feature, Not a Bug," *Nautilus*, May 2023).

And what also comes to mind at this point is the return of the brand in the most sophisticated "second-hand" items over the past decade, brought back to life by twenty-year-olds who have nothing to do with my personal memories. Not to mention the revival of the brand's great classics, gloriously emerging in the new collections in recent years. Kommers continues: "The point is that the brain does not just store inert facts which can simply be recalled or forgotten. It makes guesses about the larger conceptual story, generating assumptions and filling in the gaps as it goes—using imagination to create the whole, to build a world that we can step into." That's when it gets interesting. Suffice it to think, for instance, of the new graduable visors that juxtapose truth and fiction. But also of the "deepfakes" generated by the mechanisms of Midjourney, or of the third generation of AI applications in which you can go on a round-the-world solo voyage with Giovanni Soldini, back in 2008, or compete in a Super-G against Deborah Compagnoni, in 1992. Or else we can be projected into future and extreme universes, where a quantistic metasomething juxtaposes real people and their everyday lives (a tennis match in their club) with athletes young and old who have superficially accepted totally giving up the right to their image. The most grandiose perspective emerges here: from the "bricks" of the past the creation of an infinite future. This could lead to the return, in random order, of the greatest FILA stars ever in their most dazzling moments of athletic beauty: Marcello Guarducci, Apollonian swimmer; Madonna Grimes, the "Queen of Hip Hop"; tennis sex bomb Fabio Fognini; the ice skater Sven Kramer; the marvelous Italian long jump champion Fiona May; the fantastic Dominican-American baseball player Sammy Sosa; the most chic tennis trio of all: Gabriela Sabatini from Argentina, Monica Seles from former Yugoslavia, Karolína Plíšková from former Czechoslovakia. Not to mention the Russian tennis star Daniil Medvedev, at this point. Or Germán Silva, the Mexican marathon runner. Pure geopolitics.

That said, another matter arises: for strictly semantic reasons, the brand ambassador is also a witness. Of what? Of the fact that the brand exists, of its power and its values, which through its representation become definitively real. Magically, the athletic power of the sportsman/woman reinforces the brand and, in turn, the strength of the brand bestows added value on the person, firebranding it as a very powerful god or goddess, a member of the elite. This is one of the cornerstones of traditional anthropology: the *mana,* the passage of magic through invisible elements that transit across the contact between objects or between the person and objects. In this case, the hand that holds the racquet handle or that rearranges the catgut strings of the racquet head, the terry cloth cuff (how could we ever forget it?), the headband. All branded FILA. The pileup is crazy. And there is no need to recall how the athlete's work takes us back to the facts of our life, our own activities (not necessarily related to sports), the hard-fought victories and defeats, the dropping to one's knees and getting back up again.

The strength of the athlete is an infusion of power to face what we do not know the ending to, the adventure—incredible nevertheless—of individual existence. It should come as no surprise that the fate of many former FILA ambassadors was entrepreneurial if not political: from the Estonian Erki Nool, Olympic decathlete who then became a member of the Estonian parliament; the incredible Romanian Ion Tiriac (first an ice hockey player, then a tennis player), now a famous businessman nicknamed the "Brasov Bulldozer"; to Jamal Mashburn, a great U.S. basketball player and now the famous entrepreneur known as "Monster Mash." And so on.

Watching a game being played by great athletes also gives us power of divination. How will it end?

Place your bets. Imagine the future, of which the performer is indeed the witness, or rather the witness to a future that is still to come. Once again, pure magic. In a great show titled "Web(s) of Life" at the Serpentine Gallery in London in June 2023, the artist Tomás Saraceno, who for decades has been obsessed with spiders, their webs, and with their construction, set up in one of the gallery rooms a rather extreme ancient ritual. It concerns spiders' power of divination. The visitor can request the divination of a spider and then receive a prediction about their life or a part of their life. It is impossible, for our purposes, to think of these filaments and not go back to FILA, to the great tradition and stellar quality of the Italian textile industry. To the relationship with plant fibers, in any case, and to the exchange of different intelligences between these fibers and human beings. The ambassador is a witness to this as well. By transforming themselves into a performative dowsing totem covered in precious, ancient cotton of plant origin (let's go back to the recollection at the beginning of this essay), these ambassadors become pure power thanks precisely to the exchange. Of *mana,* of course, in this case in the form of filaments.

"Tutto fila," as the Italians say, meaning that it all makes sense in the end.

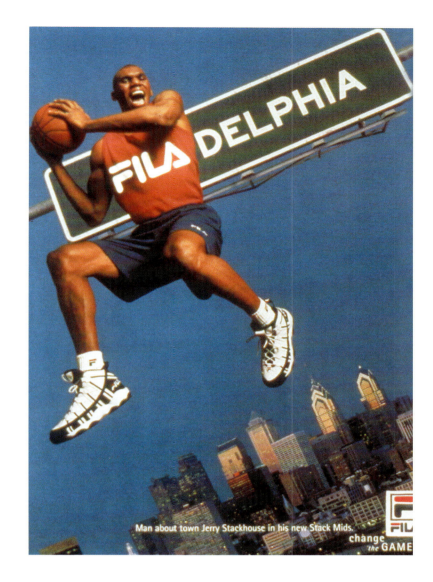

Man about town Jerry Stackhouse in his new Stack Mids.

FILA
change the GAME

EAGLES, DEVILS, GELATO: THE SECRET HISTORY OF A SHOE
Charlie Fox

MARCELLO (*designer*)
It was a long time ago, 1985? We were working on this shoe that became *something else*.

LORENZO (*designer*)
That era's another planet now. I was listening to Prince on a Walkman at my workbench; the Space Shuttle *Challenger* exploded on TV; the Cold War was *sub-zero* til Gorbachev rocked up. VCRs were the size of coffins. I mean, AIDS was new: sex was suddenly haunted and weird. You got into S & M because there wouldn't necessarily be fluids involved. Snowdrifts of coke hit the streets every morning. My nose still hurts.

LUCA (*shoemaker*)
I came from a long line of shoemakers. My grandfather, my great-grandfather and so on: all shoemakers. Probably one of my relatives is in the background of one of those St. Jerome's workshop paintings with a Giotto halo, stroking a depressed lion. But the whole tradition might have died with me if I decided to be (I don't know) a boxer or something... But I saw *The Red Shoes* on TV when I was very young. Watching Robert Helpmann playing that diabolical shoemaker who, like, enchants this girl: oh, I knew that's what I wanted to do. Make people feel wild and magical through shoes.

MARCELLO
I wasn't particularly excited about basketball as a phenomenon until one afternoon I was in a museum in Rome, and I beheld Bernini's sculpture of *Apollo and Daphne*. Suddenly it hit me that this was a basketball play in freeze frame: Apollo is hustling Daphne for the ball, much like how every defensive player in America hustled Michael Jordan, except for Apollo it's an erotic pursuit and Daphne happens to be turning into a laurel tree. Her legs are turning into bark, these strange fleshy branches are growing from her toes... I had a raspberry-chocolate gelato in a courtyard to stop my brain melting because I suddenly *understood*.

LORENZO
I was more interested in the fact that Apollo's sandal looks like a primitive version of a high top. I snuck that into the design: an allusion to antiquity. (*He laughs*.)

MARCELLO
I don't consider myself a failed sculptor. I consider the shoes sculpture. I remember seeing those Jeff Koons basketballs, eerily suspended in a kind of strange water in *Artforum*: they were profound to me as well.

LORENZO
Somehow you find your way inside it, whether it's through aesthetics or because there's a pretty girl involved: whatever. But for me, there was always something obviously transcendent about basketball. It's this strange poetry written in flesh; it looks as if it's choreographed but it's choreographed in the moment, which is a physical impossibility but they do it! "Grace" is what I mean. You can get numb to it and then the magic crashes over you in a huge wave.

MARCELLO
The early stuff was dreadful. This is a necessary part of the process, inescapable. Three weeks of failure, two weeks of boredom, one week of ecstasy: always the same and yet you never think it will be so awful, you're in this sadomasochistic relationship with your own psyche...

LORENZO
Have you ever definitively *not* had an idea? You're sitting in a McDonald's feeling like a ghost... Dante forgot to sneak that into *Purgatorio*. But slowly you find a shape you like, you make it tough, you make it loud, you get it made.

GIAN CARLO (*designer*)
You can dry-hump a concept for months and get nowhere. I invented the Godzilla Test so we wouldn't be yakking shit about Calvino and semiotics forever. Leonardo was the coffee boy: he was dumb but medically a giant. One day, I say to him, "Come, try the prototypes on, stomp around like Godzilla on a rampage." While he's crashing around to a song he likes [*I Remember Nothing* by Joy Division] we're yelling, "Does it feel *good*, Leonardo?" Dumb as he was, his instincts were impeccable: if anything passed the Godzilla Test, we knew we had a hit.

LEONARDO
I like to stomp.

LORENZO
The expenses we used to hit on Research and Development were insane. It was like having a senile grandfather who was also a fucking millionaire. The shoe that was 90 percent done. I decided me and Lorenzo had to goon a retreat to the Swiss mountains to test whether the sneaker could deal with alpine conditions. Fellini hooked us up with a satyr, we talked to him about hoof control, did some sculpting...

JEREMY (*satyr*)
I had the casts dipped in gold and I grow roses in them to this day.

MARCELLO
We should've got a picture but Fellini wanted it to be a secret, very strict.

NATHANIEL HORNBLOWER (*Swiss filmmaker and artist*)
Perhaps it was spring, a little after dawn. I was working on one of the big abstractions of which I was fond at the time [*Fantastische Schneewelt*, 1986–89), having an espresso, talking to my greyhound, Hansel, when in the hills below I see a cabin on fire: two Italian men in a state of undress running down the mountains yelling, fire, smoke, a real apocalypse...

LORENZO
I don't know how I set the cabin on fire. The important thing is I was wearing the shoes and they could handle the slopes: I *gambolled* down those hills. I think Marcello got a Polaroid of me running, which justified the whole trip and another one with that female firefighter.

MARCELLO
Yes, Steffi, the only female firefighter in that area of Switzerland...

LORENZO
Anyway, that was the expense account wanked for another week: we had tiramisu when we got back. Now it's all harried trapped-in-Kafka interns, children essentially, doing eternal image searches in between fetching coffees.

LORENZO
My favorite day is always Stress-Test Day, where you see how much damage the shoes can take... Marcello obviously wanted to get a picture of an eagle seizing the sneakers in his claws.
MARCELLO
That's the ultimate ad campaign, still: "An eagle would rather have this than his claws..." It's a beautiful fable. And they did have eagles in this special aviary on the grounds of the HQ...
ISABELLA
Somebody high up saw me destroy my boyfriend's skateboard outside a petrol station: "Come and work for us!" I had a whole garage to myself: you rub the shoes in volcanic ash, you freeze them, you bring in a hungry Doberman to eat them up and then you throw them at the wall.
LORENZO
She had beautiful hands, they looked like deer.
ISABELLA
Some of the holes were from shoes; some were from me needing to unleash aggression. I was down in this cave all day destroying things like a demon.
CORRADO (*Legal Department*)
The thing is, they're being marketed as a practical shoe, a *training* shoe. Bruno Magli doesn't have the technical problem: can you walk across ice in the dark while wearing the shoes? Can you climb over a fence easily while being chased by dogs? Yes, you can: great, sign that shit.
CHLOE (*Marketing Department*)
OK, the story of the Switzerland fire went all around the company and that gave me an idea for the campaign. *Hot sneakers*, right? We shot this commercial with Nic Roeg: a beautiful girl and a devil are making out in Hell. He slips off her top—fine; he unhooks her bra—*tutto bene*. You only see little flashes, all juicy and sweaty and lush. The devil kneels down to unlace her shoes but his claws get scorched as soon as he torches them! *Too hot*.
CORRADO
There was about as much chance of us running that campaign in a Catholic country as there is of me going out now and... riding a polar bear to Basel.
LORENZO
It was a gorgeous ad: it was *almost* porn, it was Bernini-meets-heavy metal-meets-Bosch.
LOLA (*Fellini's assistant*)
Federico, he wore those Filas for years. One night we had taken some acid—he took it a lot before *Juliet of the Spirits* and he still had a sweet tooth for it. We are walking in starlight, high, he says, "Lola, shoes are toys..."
CHLOE
We sent a pair to Basquiat but I don't know if he ever got them. I heard he was a Nike man.
MARCELLO
Once the shoes are out in the world, the angel of melancholy shrouds you in her wings. There's an absence, not unlike grief.
LORENZO
There's no signature on a shoe. Nobody ever knows who did it. But the tread goes all the way around the world and it's printed onto the pavement in blood or rain or melted ice cream: *that's* your signature, ultimately.
FEROCITY SINCLAIR (*rap historian*)
1986 was probably *the* year rap made it. Run-D.M.C. dropping *My Adidas* was a big part of that. Suddenly everybody was walking around with dollar-sign eyeballs: hip-hop equaled cash in a way it never had before. So, when Schoolly D did *Put Your Filas On* it was another example of that: hip-hop isn't only music, it's a whole mode of existence. And then people were insane for them. I remember there were riots. You were like, "For real?" That was strange back then.
DENNIS (*Custom Footwear Division*)
The biggest ones we ever made? Oh, 23s for this Baltimore kid who was a hot prospect for ten minutes until he got hit by a car. We were sent photographs. I thought I was looking at two fallen trees and then I realized, Oh, those are his *feet*! We were making sneakers for a brontosaurus.
CHLOE
The Schoolly D thing was *major*, baby: all the street boys in Milan and Rome on the corner in the sneakers came from that track being an epic smash.
LORENZO
I danced on a roof to that at 3 a.m. Loud. Almost died falling off the edge. Great memory.
CHLOE
Supernatural stuff *came* from the shoe, too. We did these little secret chats with teenagers in the park and found out an unbelievable percentage of boys and girls lost their virginity in their shoes... Like witchcraft.
LORENZO
Success is a unicorn. And once you have it, you'll feel weird and alienated anyway: believe me. The dream for every designer is that your product becomes bacterial. That might not sound like a sexy metaphor but it is the ultimate prize. They're *everywhere*. There's a cheerleader smoking in a Sofia Coppola movie and she's wearing them and the guy ahead of you in the shop hungover is wearing them... Like they always existed. All consumer products decay: they're *memento mori*, in the end. The sneakers will be in a cupboard somewhere growing fungal, you'll fall out of love with them, you'll forget them. But one afternoon, you'll pick them up and the memories of that specific afternoon where you got them, all the joy, all the possibility that is probably gone, will be encoded into the sneakers and it will break your heart.
LUCA
I still occasionally get letters from shoe fetishists saying "Thank you." You think the only shoes people will be hot for are silky ballet pumps that look like they're made from the lining of a bunny rabbit's ear and they need to be kept on hallowed pillows and brought to you by an obedient goblin. But no, people are crazy for sports shoes. Give them anybody in a nice pair of sneakers and high-thread-count sweaty socks on a summer day and, well, *miaow*. It's nice getting those fetish letters. Like getting a birthday cake from a stranger. It's just nice to know you made somebody happy.

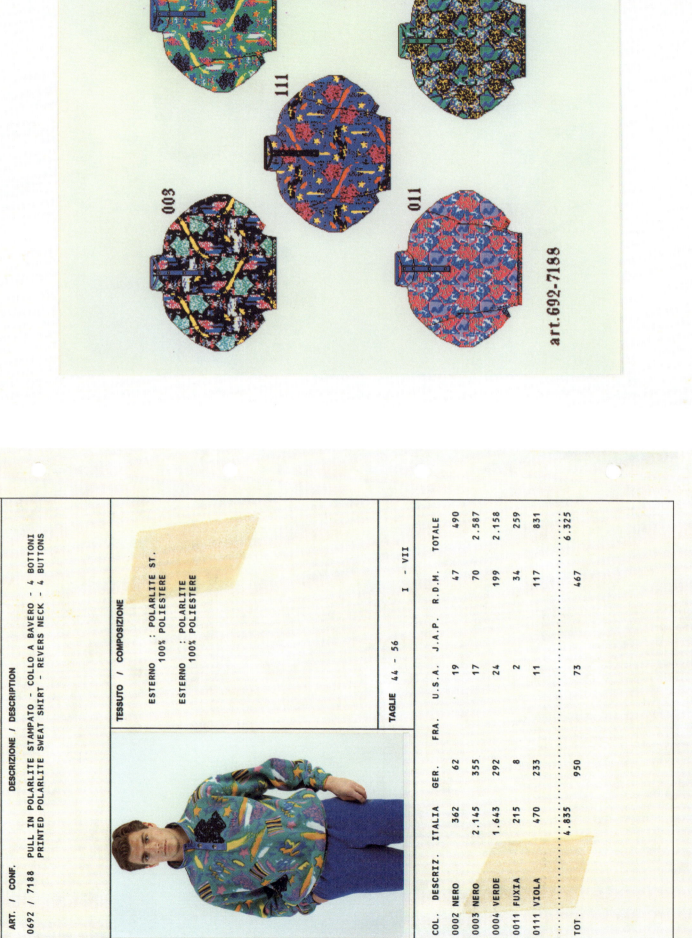

FILA SPORT S.p.A.

PAG. 81   LINEA: 03 SNOW TIME BASE

ART. / CONF.   **DESCRIZIONE / DESCRIPTION**

0692 / 7188   PULL IN POLARLITE STAMPATO - COLLO A BAVERO - 4 BOTTONI
              PRINTED POLARLITE SWEAT SHIRT - REVERS NECK - 4 BUTTONS

TESSUTO / COMPOSIZIONE

ESTERNO : POLARLITE ST.
100% POLIESTERE

ESTERNO : POLARLITE
100% POLIESTERE

TAGLIE 44 - 56   I - VII

COL.	DESCRIZ.	ITALIA	GER.	FRA.	U.S.A.	J.A.P.	R.D.M.	TOTALE
0002	NERO	362	62		19		47	490
0003	NERO	2.145	355		17		70	2.587
0004	VERDE	1.643	292		24		199	2.158
0011	FUXIA	215	8		2		34	259
0111	VIOLA	470	233		11		117	831
TOT.		4.835	950		73		467	6.325

art.692-7188

FILA SPORT S.p.A.   LINEA: 03 SNOW TIME BASE   PAG. 100

ART. / CONF.   **DESCRIZIONE / DESCRIPTION**
0684 / 3207   GIUBBOTTO CON INSERTI IN CONTRASTO, APPLICATI
JACKET CONTRASTING COLURED INSERTS

ANORAK N.

TESSUTO / COMPOSIZIONE

ESTERNO : KOREAN T.C.
 65% POLICOTTON
 POLIESTERE
 35% COTONE

FODERA : NYL|N 210T -
 100% POLIAMMIDICA

IMBOTTITURA: THERMORE
 100% POLIESTERE

TAGLIE   44 - 56
         I - VII

FONDO		INSERTI
0050 ***	001 BIANCO	1002 VIOLA-1006 INDIGO-220 GIALLO-1008 ROSS SC.
0040	362 COBALTO	1002 VIOLA-1008 ROSSO-1003 VERDINO-220 GIALLO
0051	1002 VIOLA	1004 MENTA-1006 INDIGO-001 BIANCO-1008 ROSSO SC.
0072	534 FUXIA	1006 INDIGO-220 GIALLO-1002 VIOLA-1004 MENTA
0073	400 NERO	220 GIALLO-1003 VERDINO-534 FUXIA-362 COBALTO
0085	1004 MENTA	534 FUXIA-362 COBALTO-220 GIALLO-1002 VIOLA
0178	140 BLU	130 ROSSO-001 BIANCO-362 COBALTO-362 COBALTO

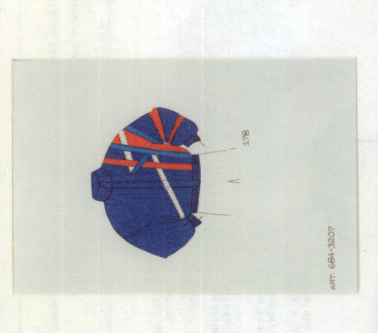

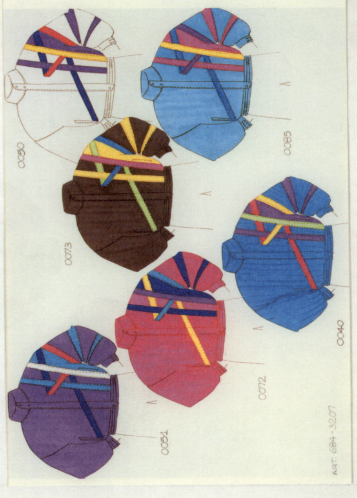

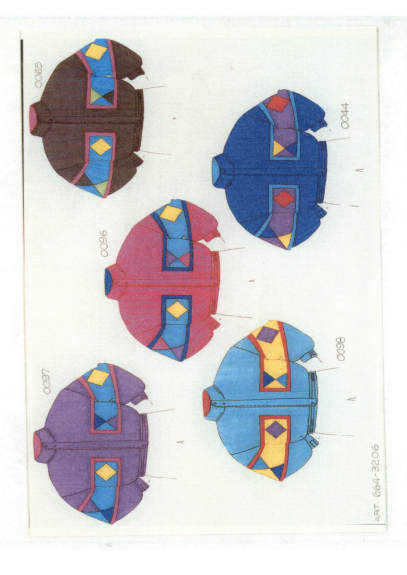

ART. 664-3206

FILA SPORT S.p.A.   LINEA : 03 SNOW TIME BASE   PAG. 97

ART. / CONF.   **DESCRIZIONE / DESCRIPTION**

0664 / 3206   GIUBBOTTO CON MOTIVI A ROMBI APPLICATI, IN CONTRASTO
JACKET WITH CONTRASTING RHOMBS MOTIF

TESSUTO / COMPOSIZIONE

ESTERNO : SUPERMICROFT
100% POLIESTERE

FODERA : NYLON 210T
100% POLIAMMIDICA

IMBOTTITURA : THERMORE
100% POLIESTERE

TAGLIE   44 - 56
I - VII

	FONDO	INT.COLLO	INSERTI
0097 ***	1002 VIOLA	534 FUXIA	1004 MENTA-1002 V.LA-1006 IND.-220 GIAL
0044	1006 INDACO	1004 MENTA	1002 V.LA-1006 IND.-220 GIAL.-1008 ROSS
0065	400 NERO	534 FUXIA	1007 TURCH.-400 NERO-1003 VER.-220 GIAL
0096	534 FUXIA	1006 INDACO	1004 MENTA-534 FUX.-1002 V.LA 220 GIALL
0098	1004 MENTA	1008 ROSSO	220 GIAL.-1004 MENTA-1006 IND.-1002V.LA

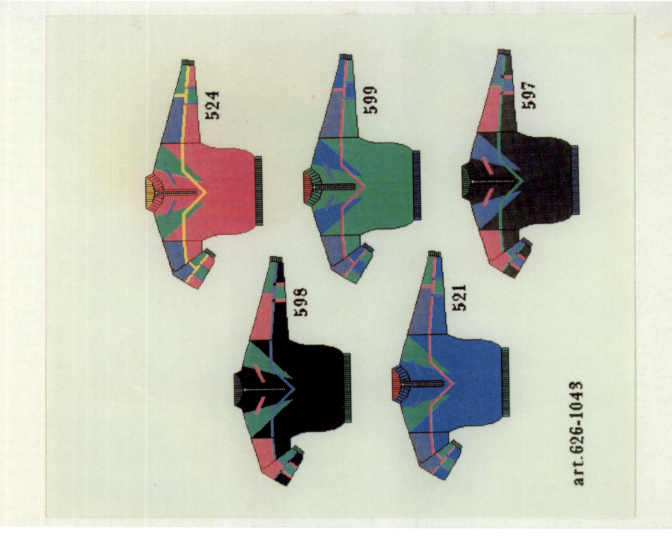

FILA SPORT S.p.A.
PAG. 23

LINEA : 03 SNOW TIME BASE

ART. / CONF.	DESCRIZIONE / DESCRIPTION
0626 / 1043	PULL TECNICO JACQUARD COLLO LUPETTO CON ZIP MISTO LANA
	JACQUARD TURTLENECK WITH ZIP

TESSUTO / COMPOSIZIONE

ESTERNO :
50% LANA
50% ACRILICA

TAGLIE 44 - 56   I - VII

COL.	DESCRIZ.	ITALIA	GER.	FRA.	U.S.A.	J.A.P.	R.D.M.	TOTALE
0521	INDIGO							
0524	FUXIA							
0597	GRIGIO SC.	14						14
0598	BLU	14						14
0599	VERDE							
	TOT.	28						28

art.626-1043

FILA SPORT S.p.A.

LINEA: 03 SNOW TIME BASE   PAG. 58

ART. / CONF.   **DESCRIZIONE / DESCRIPTION**

0626 / 3104   PULLOVER GIROCOLLO TECNICO JACQUARD CON CERNIERA
             PULLOVER ROUND NECK, JACQUARD WITH ZIP

TESSUTO / COMPOSIZIONE

ESTERNO: FILATO 2/25 A 2 CAPI
          50% LANA
          50% ACRILICA

TAGLIE   44 - 56
           I - VII

	FONDO	SPALLONE	DISEGNO
0168 ***	362 COBALTO	923 VIOLA	002BIANCO-347BLUCINA-923VIOLA
0174	362 COBALTO	140 BLU	130ROSSO-002BIANCO-140BLU
0175	923 VIOLA	347 BLUCINA	322GIALLO-371VERDE-347BLUCINA
0176	347 BLU CINA	534 FUXIA	371VERDE-923VIOLA-534FUXIA

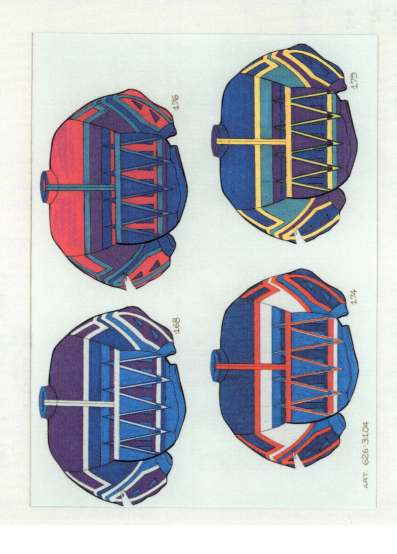

ART. 626-3104

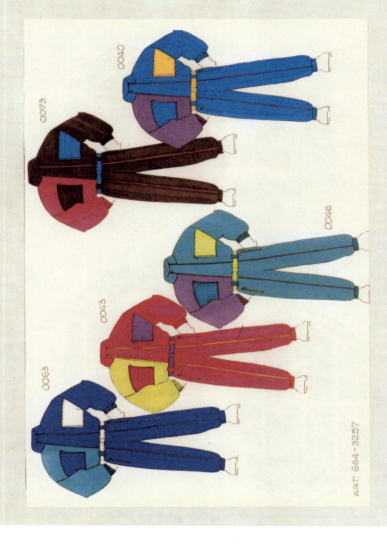

ART. 664-3257

FILA SPORT S.p.A.

LINEA: 03 SNOW TIME BASE   **PAG.** 132

ART. / CONF.   **DESCRIZIONE / DESCRIPTION**
0664 / 3257   TUTA CON INSERTI-2 ZIP DAVANTI PER APERTURA TOTALE
OVERALLS WITH INSERTS - 2 ZIP ON FRONT FOR OPENING

TESSUTO / COMPOSIZIONE

ESTERNO   :SUPERMICROFT
100% POLIESTERE

FODERA   :NYLON 210T
100% POLIAMMIDICA

IMBOTTITURA :THERMORE T37
100% POLIESTERE

TAGLIE 44 - 56
I - VII

	FONDO	INSERTI	FODERA
0063 ***	1006 INDIGO	1004 MENTA-001 BIANCO	1004 MENTA
0040	362 COBALTO	1002 VIOLA-220 GIALLO	1002 VIOLA
0043	534 FUXIA	1003 VERDINO-1002 VIOLA	1002 VIOLA
0046	1004 MENTA	1002 VIOLA-1003 VERDINO	1002 VIOLA
0073	400 NERO	534 FUXIA-362 COBALTO	534 FUXIA

FILA SPORT S.p.A.

LINEA: 03 SNOW TIME BASE **PAG.** 90

ART. / CONF.	DESCRIZIONE / DESCRIPTION
0674 / 3236	GIUBBOTTO UNITO CON POLAR STAMPATO INTERNO REVERSIBILE
	JACKET, PLAIN COLOUR, PRINTED POLAR, REVERSIBLE INSIDE

ANORAK REVERSIBLE

TESSUTO / COMPOSIZIONE	
ESTERNO	: SUPERMICROFT
	100% POLIESTERE
INTERNO	: POLAR ST.ART.PK718
	100% POLIESTERE

TAGLIE 44 - 56
I - VII

	FONDO		INTERNO POLAR STAMPATO	
0060 ***	1003	VERDINO	9993	VERDE/NERO
0061	400	NERO	9992	FUXIA/NERO
0062	1002	VIOLA	9992	FUXIA/NERO
0155	130	ROSSO	9993	VERDE/NERO
0156	362	COBALTO	9993	VERDE/NERO
0157	140	BLU	9993	VERDE/NERO
0158	1006	INDIGO	9993	VERDE/NERO
0159	1004	MENTA	9992	FUXIA/NERO
0160	220	GIALLO	9993	VERDE/NERO
0161	1008	ROSSO SC.	9993	VERDE/NERO

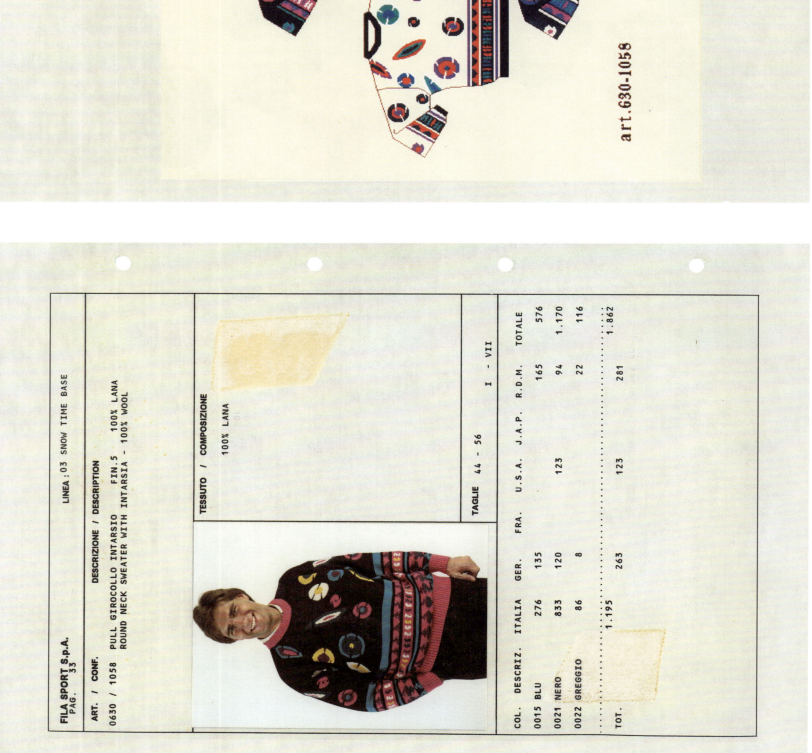

FILA SPORT S.p.A.
PAG. 33

LINEA : 03 SNOW TIME BASE

ART. / CONF.	DESCRIZIONE / DESCRIPTION
0630 / 1058	PULL GIROCOLLO INTARSIO FIN.5 100% LANA
	ROUND NECK SWEATER WITH INTARSIA - 100% WOOL

TESSUTO / COMPOSIZIONE

100% LANA

TAGLIE 44 - 56   I - VII

COL.	DESCRIZ.	ITALIA	GER.	FRA.	U.S.A.	J.A.P.	R.D.M.	TOTALE
0015	BLU	276	135				165	576
0021	NERO	833	120		123		94	1.170
0022	GREGGIO	86	8				22	116
TOT.		1.195	263		123		281	1.862

art.630-1058

MODERN TRADITION: A TIMELESS LOGO
Emanuele Coccia

A logo has nothing to do with the expression of a pure commercial intention. It is a much older and more complex cultural expression than what we usually associate with it. In fact, each logo implies a tacit classification of the order of objects around us and presupposes a decision about the role that different types of artifacts should and can play in the mutual relationship we have with other human beings. Each logo initiates for us the conversations and interactions we can weave with and together with them and does so before any of our gestures, before any of our words. Therefore, to understand the meaning, weight, and nature of the logo of a brand like FILA, it is necessary to start very far back. The red and blue monogram invented by Sergio Privitera in 1973 and then perfected over the years indicates much more than the industrial origin of a garment or its economic value.

There is first of all the nature of the objects on which this mark is inscribed. Whether it is clothing or accessories, the pieces of clothing that we confuse with our skin have a very peculiar meaning.

For centuries we measured our technical progress in our relationship with stones. Indeed, stones seemed to be the first and only witness to the human capacity to modify reality and the surrounding environment: the hardest, most durable of materials is what defined the intensity of our strength and ingenuity with which the human species was able to reduce the world to its needs. It is hard not to grasp the mythological and Promethean dimensions of this strange primordial scene: the human being alone before the stone, as if there were no other living beings with whom it had been necessary to forge alliances to improve the reality of the world, and as if the world itself was an immense desert that could never console our loneliness. Perhaps this is also why technology, as the embodiment of stone and its manipulation, was an immediate synonym for war: the first ordinary tools were first and foremost weapons. Such a view, which had been systematized since the mid-nineteenth century by the British archaeologist John Lubbock and led to the distinction between the Paleolithic and Neolithic eras, stemmed from more than one misunderstanding and generated a thousand others. The methodological assumption was a positivist and somewhat blind adherence to the remaining archaeological material: the earliest material evidence from prehistoric times that we have are indeed stones and later metals. But this is so only because the first objects that individuals belonging to our species produced were of organic origin and could not withstand the grip of time. Probably, more than the manufacture of weapons it was the weaving of clothes that engaged the technical imagination of our ancestors. Weaving is much older than hunting. And it is for the same reason that, as feminist-inspired history has suggested, women played a far more important role than has long been imagined in the invention of technology. It is that, after all, which many of the myths elaborated in the Mediterranean area seem to thematize. Thus in the myths of the Semitic area that are crystallized for us in the Hebrew Tanakh and the Christian Old Testament, clothes are the objects that mark the transition for humankind from an existence that does not need technology (a *bios atechnos*, as the ancient commentators wrote) to technical life: clothes made from fig leaves or tunics produced through skins are the first artifacts to appear in the lives of Adam and Eve. This is no small detail: it means that if we take this myth literally, it is to a garment, to an object of yarn that we must ask to explain what technology is.

On the other hand, the Greco-Roman myth of Arachne makes weaving the ground where humanity, led by a woman, challenges and defeats by technical prowess the gods themselves and subjects them to bitter humiliation. Again, the myth is far from insignificant: every time we weave we are taking our nature beyond its own boundaries.

To talk about textiles, yarns, the artifacts that result from them, and their modernity does not mean—as it can happen with many of the objects that have accompanied the lives of Western societies since the Industrial Revolution—to talk about secondary and relatively marginal accessories. Instead, it means talking about objects that define the boundaries of our very nature: companions of life for so long (thousands of years) that they now blend in with our face. Socks, shoes, and T-shirts are the most universal and most social objects: everyone wears them, every day, all day. To place a mark on these objects is to give an identity to our lives more than to a tiny portion of them. The universality —historically, geographically, and demographically— which such objects bear is absolutely incomparable.

On the other hand, sport is the place where bodies seek and find the forms of expression of their deepest freedom. It is no coincidence that, for example, the liberation of the female body that occurred at the dawn of contemporary fashion with Coco Chanel took place precisely through the adoption of sportswear transfigured into elegant forms. At a time when women were barely free and could participate in very few sports, Chanel thus suggested that to understand what femininity is, one must ask what is a body free to move anywhere. Sportswear, then, has always been the place where each society has wanted to mark and make visible this freedom open to anyone. Giving a FILA dress a visible identity, therefore, meant finding the formula for this liberation at hand.

After all, freedom and universality have been fundamental elements of the brand's identity. Unlike many of its competitors, FILA has always been characterized by an incredible commercial and cultural transversality: one did not have to belong to a class or age group to wear a FILA garment; it was enough to possess the desire for freedom. The FILA garment merely transfigured this same desire into a symbol of restrained and discreet elegance. The consequences of these premises are clear: the logo was thus not to serve to distinguish but to unite and find the lowest common denominator among ages, social and economic classes, ethnic or national cultural identities. It was not to create an additional identity that it was impossible to get rid of; it was a common sign that had to be able to be resigned as easily as it could be adopted.

In those very years, moreover, U.S. marketing theory was finally freeing itself from the ideas (first expressed by Thorstein Veblen at the end of the nineteenth century) that had guided it for decades: that consumption was an arena for distinction and that everything worn should express a form of snobbery, a desire to assert one's superiority over others. As would be formulated by marketing thinking in the late 1970s and early 1980s, branding was rather to express the air of family among the objects purchased and, above all, belonging to a common way of life, shared by many.

These guidelines are perfectly respected. Already the choice of shape and colors testifies to this. The logo was born in 1973, at the height of the psychedelic explosion for acidic, fluorescent hues and the return of a rich, decorative, baroque style—that of, among others, Milton Glaser, or that of Seymour Chwast and his magazine *Push Pin*, which had revisited the late nineteenth-century aesthetic in a libertarian and anarchic key. In the same years, DIY culture exploded in the United States and with it the destruction of the modernist graphic order: the famous book *Adhocism* by Charles Jencks and Nathan Silver came out in 1972, the same year in which Robert Venturi, Denise Scott Brown, and Steven Izenour published *Learning from Las Vegas* and made architecture the explosion of diverse and contradictory symbols. In that same year, John Berger launched the BBC television series *Ways of Seeing* and published the book of the same name that forever crumbled the illusion of formalist neutrality that modernist typography (especially Swiss and German typography) had long cultivated: forms are always loaded with history and are politically anything but neutral.

Privitera's choice is in clear countertrend. Unlike many similar brands (just take the example of Lacoste's crocodile or Ralph Lauren's horse or even the Olympic clover that Adidas welcomed into its logo in those very years) there are no animals, plants, or figures. Nor are there any references to the counterculture of the time, to the thrusts toward liberation, as in the two young men leaning on each other's backs of the almost coeval brand of Robe di Kappa, designed by Maurizio Vitale in 1969. In the most dense, tense, and violent moment of Italian history, the one between the youth revolt of 1968 and the so-called "Years of Lead" that would explode in 1977, FILA chooses the neutral typographic purity of the 1920s and 1930s, the one considered as a form of liberation from any useless decorative waste by El Lissitzky or Jan Tschichold. The choice of colors is also part of the desire for non-distinction: blue and red are among the most traditional. Just think of K-Way, which was born a decade earlier, or Pepsi, which had adopted this color pair since the 1950s, and of course the visual identity of the London Underground. It was again about expressing a modernity that was discreet and effective, not excessive, efficient.

The artistic inspirations that seem to underlie the lettering go in the same direction. The early 1970s are the mature art years of Sol LeWitt and Donald Judd. Robert Smithson, a flagship figure of Land Art, dies in 1973, the same year of a major retrospective of conceptual artist Joseph Kosuth. In Italy the figures associated with Arte Povera, which had emerged from the famous exhibition in Amalfi in 1968, had disrupted the plastic and visual universe. The choice to refer to Robert Indiana, author of the famous *Love* sculpture and expressive of a much more consensual and mainstream art, is certainly not accidental. Privitera seems to be formulating a line that is as universal as possible, one that avoids and blunts the explosive tensions of the culture of those years.

Similarly, it is no coincidence that the first great sports hero with whom the brand identified was Björn Borg, the perfect embodiment of success without idiosyncrasies, produced by talent and will, a million light years away from the rebellious, elusive, and unstoppable spirit of his eternal rival John McEnroe. "Tennis is a traditional game," Borg is told to have said. "A big sport like tennis does not need too many changes." Through the F-Box, Privitera makes modernity and tradition rhyme. After all, there is no true freedom if it is not rooted in some form of deep nature: and to talk about clothing, as mentioned above, is to discuss anthropology rather than design. The logo and its variations succeed in inventing a form of the classic. And it is this miracle, which seems to reconcile history and innovation, that, ever since, characterizes the history of the whole brand.

Snow Time Fila 1978 per cambiare la neve.

CLOTHING AND ACCESSORIES 1991

CLOTHING AND ACCESSORIES 1991

CLOTHING AND ACCESSORIES 1991

CLOTHING AND ACCESSORIES 1991

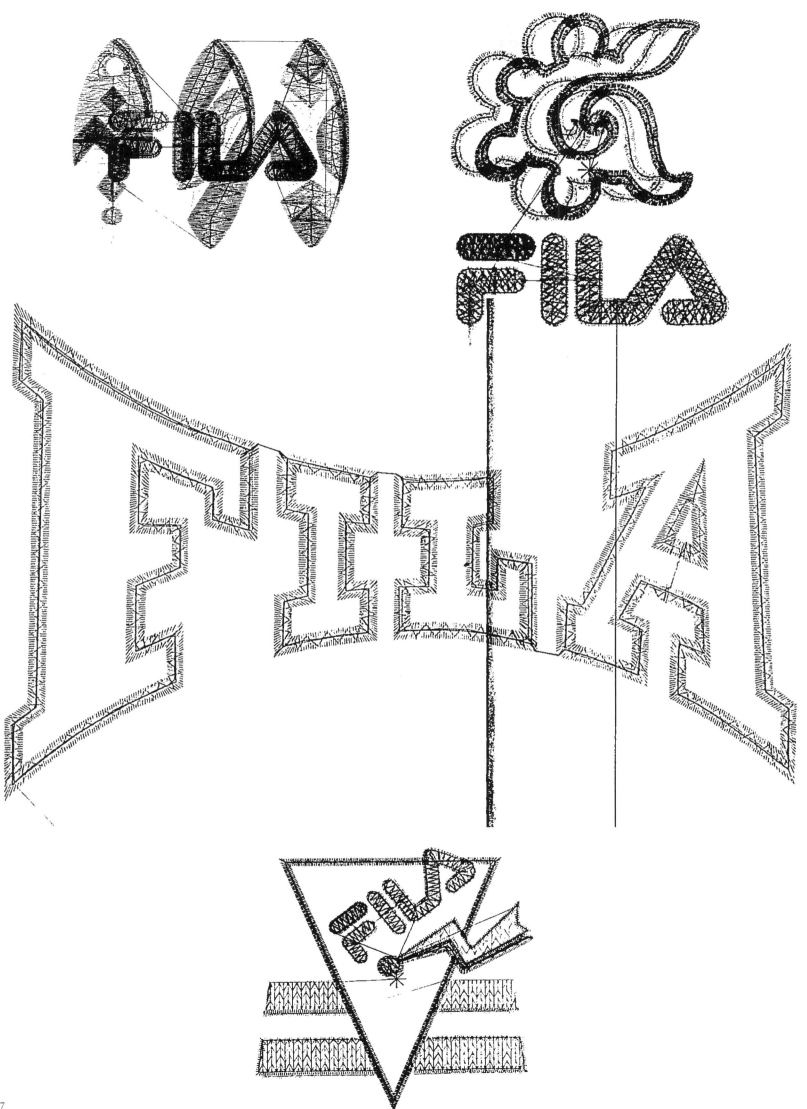

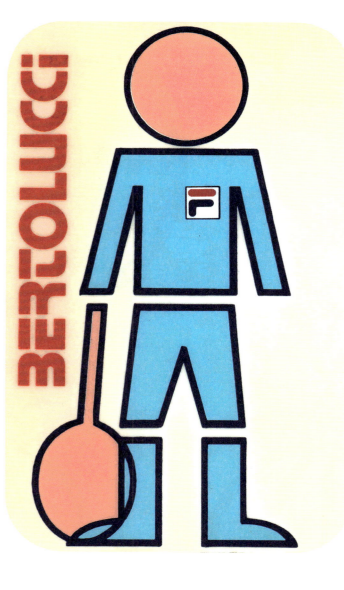

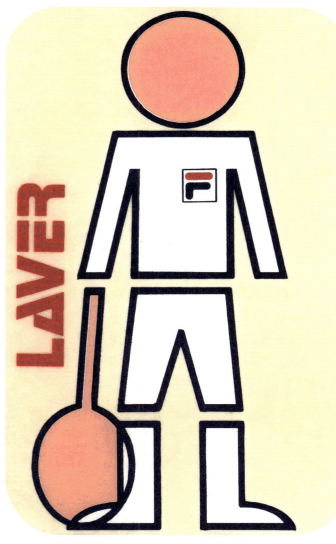

FILA FOR TENNIS

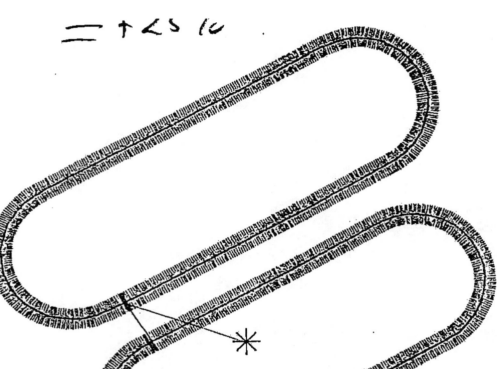

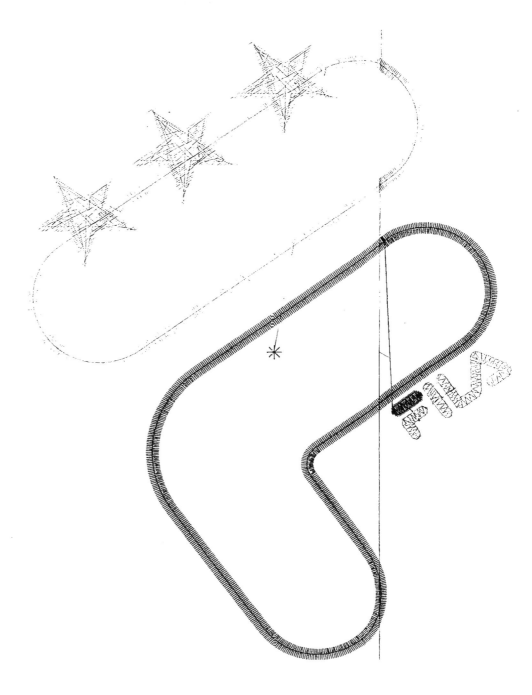

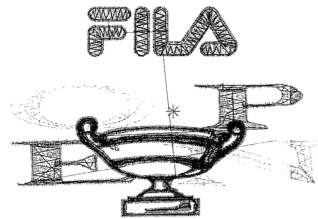

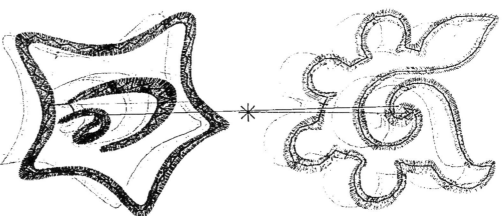

Now for a story that begins with a C
L
I
F
F
H
A
N
G
E
R

REINHOLD MESSNER × FILA

Hanging on by threads.

Reinhold Messner had spent so much time living on the edge, to write his life story, you'd need a pen in one hand and a pick axe in the other to accurately convey it.

He holds a conversation with the same sort of GRIP as he does a mountain-side. You get the feeling that if you don't hang on to his every word, you might die from the fall.

"The relationship with FILA was special for working people," says Messner, speaking of Dr. Enrico Frachey's, the then director, and his (Messner's) long-standing collaboration.

IN TERMS OF MOUNTAIN RANGES, THEIRS WAS PERHAPS THE MOST IMPRESSIVE

On his first first solo up the treacherous wall of Nanga Parbat, an 8,000 meter jaunt, Messner speaks of the real danger. **Mountain-eers should be seen, not hurt.**

"Getting lost in that altitude means being lost forever," Messner says. "And I could STAND OUT in these FILA garments."

166

He holds his beliefs with the grip strength of someone who's pinched Mt. Everest's cheeks, and lived to make her blush.

" For a long time now, we have used fleece; it was all synthetic polyester. Now, we change and use old things that are recycled and are used maybe longer than a garment before."

Mountaineering is often a solitary act. Messner is, therefore, probably one of the world's greatest antisocial climbers, walking his own path.

Going counter to the world. Creating something that lasts —perhaps, even something that lasts longer than a lifetime. A legacy. A story that can be told and retold again.

And if there's any hill worth dying on, maybe that's the one.

"CHANGE THE GAME" – FILA AND THE EVOLUTION OF ADVERTISING FROM THE 1970s TO THE 2000s
Michele Galluzzo

A GREAT NAME
The year 1973 was a watershed for what had been described in the advertising pages until a few years before as "one of the greatest and most import ant Italian knitwear companies": Fratelli Fila SpA industries. This was just over sixty years from when the company, operating in the weaving and carding of combed wools, was founded in the city of Biella, after having undertaken, in the mid-1920s, the production of knitwear for men, women, and children. This followed a period of strong growth in the 1950s and the group's subsequent division into three parts—Filatura, Lanificio, and Maglificio Biellese. The company reached the 1970s marked by several moments of crisis. So by the time 1973 rolled around, the company management realized that the time had come to explore new markets and to further diversify production. To do so properly it also understood that its advertising communication had to be diversified and renewed.

The early 1970s were thus a turning point. In the world of Italian advertising this period coincides with what the trade press explicitly defined as a "schism" —a coming apart between the graphic designers and the world of advertising. American-type ad agencies definitively imposed themselves—i.e. full service, marketing-oriented, or creative; the graphic artists were no longer the undisputed key players. It was in 1973 that Franco Grignani, one of the protagonists of the first season of modern Italian advertising and graphic art, the author of one of the most famous symbols of popular world culture—the logo for pure virgin wool—stated that "advertising, in the way it has arrived today, marginalizes graphic art. [...] Graphic art, where it still intervenes, [...] is not as evident as it was, as essential to the ad composition [...]."

At that time, most Italian graphic designers increasingly saw themselves as being more in the tradition of industrial design and part of the vision of the designer as a problem solver and the director of complex systems for creating a visual identity. This resulted in graphic designers creating fewer ads and more visual identity guidelines, logos, and corporate identity manuals. It was precisely at that moment of rupture between graphic design and advertising that FILA metamorphosed, and it did so by going in the opposite direction—that is, by entrusting to one person the design of the new logo and the art direction of the new advertising approach: Sergio Privitera, consultant for FILA from the spring of 1972 to the fall of 1974.

The shift embraced by the management at FILA and the double track on which communications were moving at this time of transition can clearly be seen in two of the Biella brand's commercial communications leaflets.

The first is a front-and-back promotional poster: written in white Grotesk font are the words "FILA un grande nome"; the visual part of the poster, on both sides, is occupied by photographs of children, adolescents, twenty-year-olds, ordinary youths portrayed wearing some of the label's knitwear items as they enjoy relaxing together outdoors on the grass. The ones paged by Privitera resemble the frames of photographic reportage in poster format that encapsulates the escapist spirit or experiences of reappropriation of the outdoor world that was being experienced in those years by both the extra-parliamentary left-wing communes and the workshops of the radical designers. This poster can be read as the soft and natural evolution of the Maglificio Biellese Fila that, between the 1950s and 1960s, produced clothing labeled Fila, Maby, and Pierre Cardin. Confirming that continuity, the company's historical logo is visible: the letters that spell FILA are arranged in an arch in which the letter "F" stretches downward and points directly at the center of a geometrically synthetized globe.

The second graphic object designed by Privitera in 1974 is an ad inaugurating the new season described above: the birth of a revolutionary collection designed by Pierluigi Rolando and Alessandro Galliano—respectively the artistic director and the technical director—called White Line. Inspired by the white lines on tennis courts, the line actually introduces into the tennis context, which was dominated by the color white, new colors like blue and red. And precisely these two colors define the layout of the ad: the blue used for the color of the background, and the red that especially stands out on the cardigan worn by Adriano Panatta portrayed on the cover.

The two-color code introduced by White Line can also be found in another element that marks a break from the past. Visible next to the historical FILA logo, in a sequence of squares that describe the hierarchies of the parent company at a time of transition, is the new FILA label—an 'F' made up of a red line and a blue line—the result of a conversation between Privitera himself and the team working inside the company.

However much the genealogy of the new label nicknamed "F-Box" may be clear, it is interesting to note how, to compose the logotype of the "Linea Panatta" appearing in the ad, Privitera chose the Stop typeface designed by Aldo Novarese for a historical type foundry located less than 80 kilometers from the Biella company, the Nebiolo company of Turin. Upon closer examination, Novarese's Stop typeface, in addition to offering the word "Panatta" the appearance of a complete logo, also seemed to be echoed in the stencil "F" of the new FILA logo. Stop, after all, had been launched in the early 1970s as a display alphabet capable of offering graphic designers and typographers the chance to easily produce "brands, logos, and monograms."

The presence in Privitera's advertising campaign of photographs of famous athletes like Adriano Panatta, Rod Laver, and Ion Tiriac bears witness to another important change in the company's communications strategy. From this moment onward, in fact, the renewed FILA label would constantly represent its production by using outstanding endorsements from the world of tennis first of all, and sports more generally in the years to come.

CREATIVITY AND SPORTS
During the same years when the White Line was introduced to the market with photographs of famous athletes, the Biella brand was promoted on the pages of ads with models, both men and women, shown posing, based on a type of photography influenced more by the world of fashion advertising and publishing than by that of sports. The shift was especially guided by the Montenegro-born photographer Čedomir Komljenović, better known as Monty Shadow. Backed by his experience in the Condé Nast editorial group's London headquarters, Monty Shadow accompanied the evolutions and the combinations of the brand on and off the courts, turning FILA into one of the brands of reference on the "athleisure" scene in the years to come. The influence of the photographer's gaze can be found in the long exposures used in 1977 by the photographer Luciano Buglioni to emphasize the dynamism of the model/tennis player, the wide angle chosen in 1979 to slenderize the bodies in the snow in the "FILA for Skiing" campaign, and in many of the shots directed by the Twen Studio the following year for the international campaign "Creatività e Sport" (Creativity and Sports).

The keyword was creativity. Already appearing in 1975 at the bottom of ads or as a tagline was the expression "La Creatività nello Sport" (Creativity in Sports). The verbal repetition inevitably harkened back to the American "creative revolution" that in the 1960s had invested the world of Madison Avenue advertising agencies, and that starting from the following decade would also begin to consolidate on the Italian advertising scene, offering communication based on irony and self-irony, where the reader's active role was to decipher and decode the message. Advertising photographers—as well as graphic designers and illustrators—increasingly conversed with the "creative duos" consisting of the art director and the copywriter, breathing life into examples of collective authorship.

The Italian creative revolution was also intercepted by the Biella brand, which in the early 1980s started collaborating with the Milanese headquarters of the American agency Leo Burnett, managing to bring together extremely refined art and copy. The collaboration between the art direction of Agostino Reggio and the texts by Paolo del Bravo produced an advertising page that was visually experimental, in which the computerized image of the parabola of a tennis ball revealed the innovative use of graphite in the "Champion" tennis racket. On the contrary, in 1982, an almost empty page featured the realistic illustration of four mountains—the work of Luisa Raini—topped by a headline—signed Alessandro Baldoni—that stated: "Un annuncio pubblicitario poetico in omaggio all'incredibile Reinhold Messner e alla sua tuta FILA che quest'anno hanno scalato quasi 32 mila metri" (A poetic ad in homage to the amazing Reinhold Messner and his FILA tracksuit, both of them this year climbing almost 32,000 meters).

In addition to the creative advertising and that featuring photography well in tune with the contemporary trends, FILA continued to express itself through the sponsorship of sports celebrities as well, including Björn Borg, Andrea Jaeger, John McEnroe, Guillermo Vilas, Paolo Bertolucci, Evonne Goolagong, the Olympic champion Hanni Wenzel, and the Ferrari racing driver Didier Pironi. This continued into the 1990s, with big names like Jennifer Capriati, Monica Seles, and Boris Becker.

FILA's sports endorsements ended up literally composing the multidisciplinary and international mosaic visible on many advertising pages promoting its production in the first two decades of the birth of the new brand, also inaugurating the entrance into the market of sports shoes, with the launch in 1983 of the model FX-3 Original Tennis.

The photographic compositions with the company's ambassadors paged in a grid by the B&S agency definitively made way for the disruption of the grid and the advent of postmodernism. The symptoms of this change can especially be found in the advertising inaugurating the Piedmontese company's arrival on the American basketball scene in the early 1990s. "Change the game," read the payoff. There was a mixing up of the fonts, styles, of the sizes of the different letters, the definitive abandonment of the two-tone red and blue, and the free and dynamic arrangement of the texts in the space of the page. It was also the advent of increasingly digital and computerized aesthetics, and the opening in 1997 of the company domain www.fila.com.

Floating around on the scene were basketball players like Grant Hill, Jamal Mashburn, Hersey Hawkins, Jerry Stackhouse. The latter appeared in an iconic ad where the Sixers' guard jumped and created a mash-up between the Piedmont company's logotype and the sign on the highway of the largest city in Pennsylvania so that it read "Fila-delphia."

"FEEL," "LIFE," "FUN"
In 1976, just two years after the birth of the F-Box logo, the company adopted a logotype that it is still using today. Starting from an "F" with the red "biscotto" (the red stripe on top with rounded corners), the Japanese designer Imai Hironobu created the wordmark FILA, which from that moment onward would be associated with the label previously designed by the team inside the company with Privitera's collaboration.

The new FILA lettermark—which would be called "Linear"—associated with the label inside the square, would instantly play a key role in both the clothing and the ads. Whereas in the campaigns from the mid-1970s the F-Box played the leading role on the pages thanks to the photographic rendering of the label or the patch present on the clothing, the logotype designed by Imai would soon evolve into a veritable FILA alphabet, functional to the construction of collection logos (Sportime Watches in 1987, FILA Golf in 1992), lettering for events (the FILA Trophy Tournament in Milan in 1985), publications (the magazine for the US market *F.Y.I.*). The FILA alphabet, also visible in the headlines "Feel," "Life," "Fun" connoting the 2007 spring campaign, over the years would become so characteristic of the brand's visual identity and advertising communications that it would end up being faked, forged, cited, and appropriated more or less legitimately by the real world. But on the other hand, when successful advertising communication enters popular culture it becomes a common asset, a shared language.

Che cosa è la cintura NOBELT??

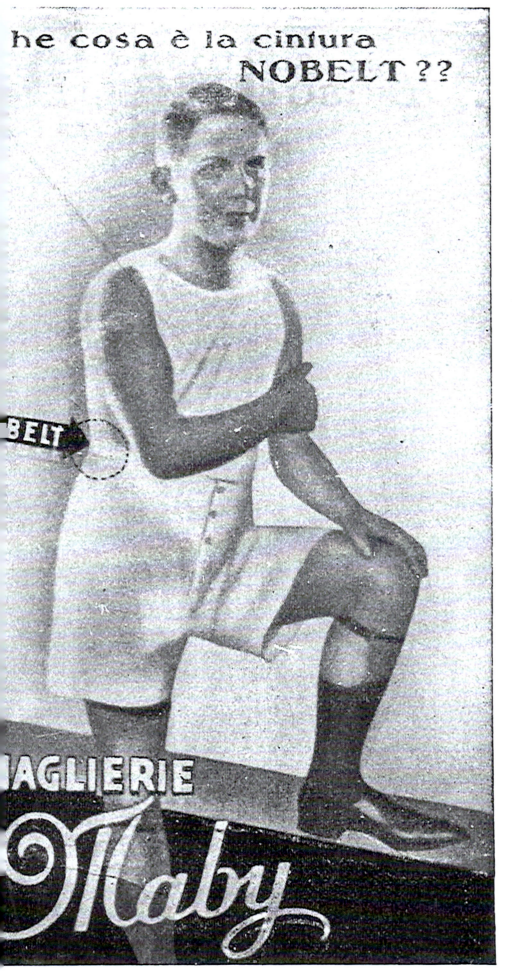

MAGLIERIE Maby

La NOBELT è una striscia di un sottile foglio di gomma pura; essa è sottoposta a tensione solamente quando è portata, ed è trattata con procedimento speciale per impedire OGNI DETERIORAMENTO CONSEGUENTE ALLA LAVATURA E BOLLITURA.

GARANZIA: Tutte le applicazioni NOBELT che non rispondessero ai requisiti di cui sopra, verranno senz'altro ritirate e sostituite.

MAGLIEFICIO BIELLESE BIELLA

The Allegro Collection

(A bona fide limited edition)

For the lady who appreciates the very best.

The entire hardware package is totally coordinated with a series of elegant bags and headcovers. Be the first to obtain this very distinctive and exciting collection.

The ultimate in playability and the epitome of great looks. A beautifully designed flow-weighted clubhead in conjunction with a very responsive graphite shaft, specifically created by Unifiber, U.S.A. for the demands of the ladies golf swing. FILA GOLF'S response to fashion/function in a very upscale market.

Color, color, and more color. The set is tastefully matched component by component. The paint fill in the clubhead complements the custom shaft and grip.

Golf Equipment and Accessories

Licensed by Fila Sport S.p.A
Biella, Italy

FILA GO

Renaissance Golf Produ
5812 Machine Drive
Huntington Beach, CA 92649
714-897-8213 • 800-325-4399
FAX 714-897-7908

LIFE

YOU'RE AS GOOD AS YOU FILA®

CHANGE THE GAME

FILA

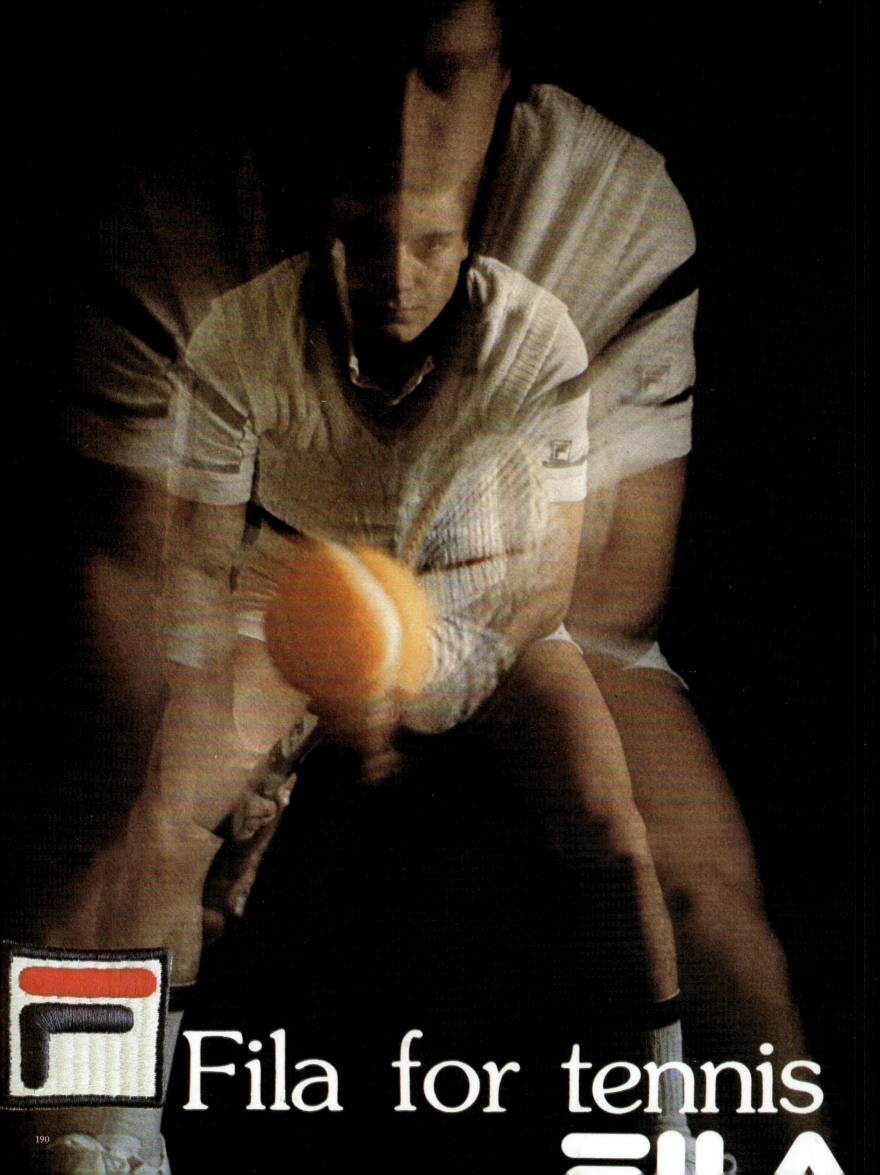

Fila Light

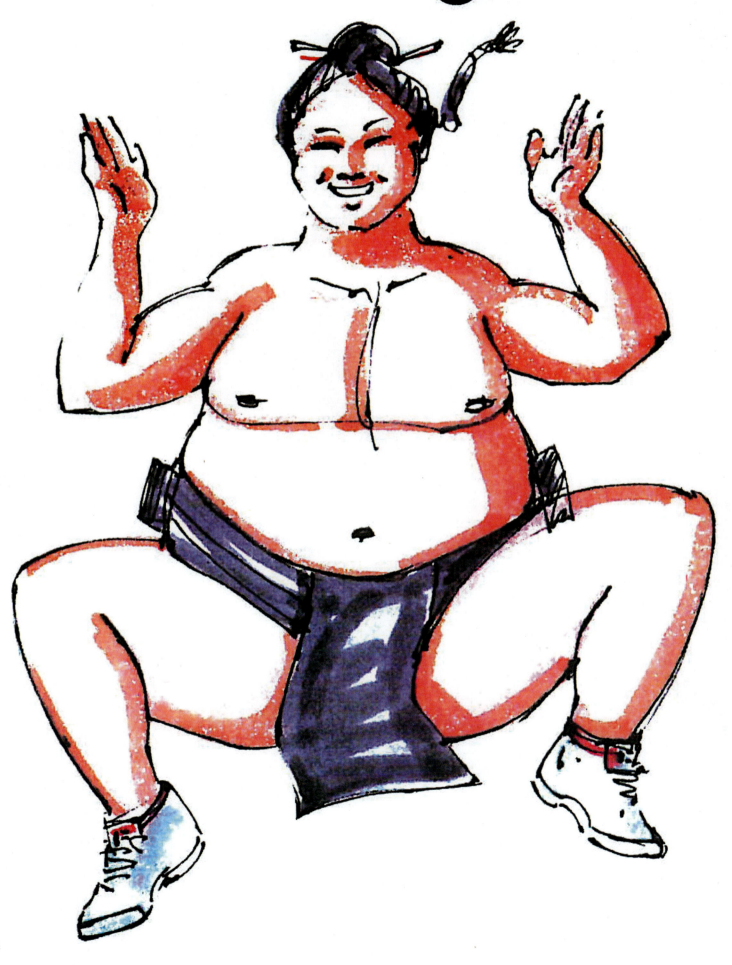

FILA GOLF

Men's Fila Model Woods.
These woods feature a high toe and low heel weight distribution built into the core. This system, much like the Fila Iron, produces the ultimate feel and playability. The face is referenced off the leading edge of the hosel producing a dead square set from the driver down through the seven wood. Investment cast from 17-4 stainless steel and manufactured with infinite care.

Men's Fila Model Iron
This iron features blended back cavity that place weight high on the toe and low the heel, producing superior perfo mance and the most solid feeling iron golf. The set has a minimal progressiv offset to accommodate players of all ski levels. Made from investment cast ing quality 17-4 stainless steel, finished with unique bright pewter polish and crafted wit Fila's traditional attention to detai

This iron was recently tested by a independent laboratory against th two leading sellers. The Fila iro was superior in distance an dispersion

<u>Quality you demand,</u>
<u>performance you</u>
<u>deserve.</u>

FILA GOLF

Renaissance Golf Products, Inc.
5812 Machine Drive, Huntington Beach, CA 9264
714-897-8213 • 800-325-4399 • FAX 714-897-79

Golf Equipment and Accessories
Licensed by Fila Sport S.p.A.
Biella, Italy

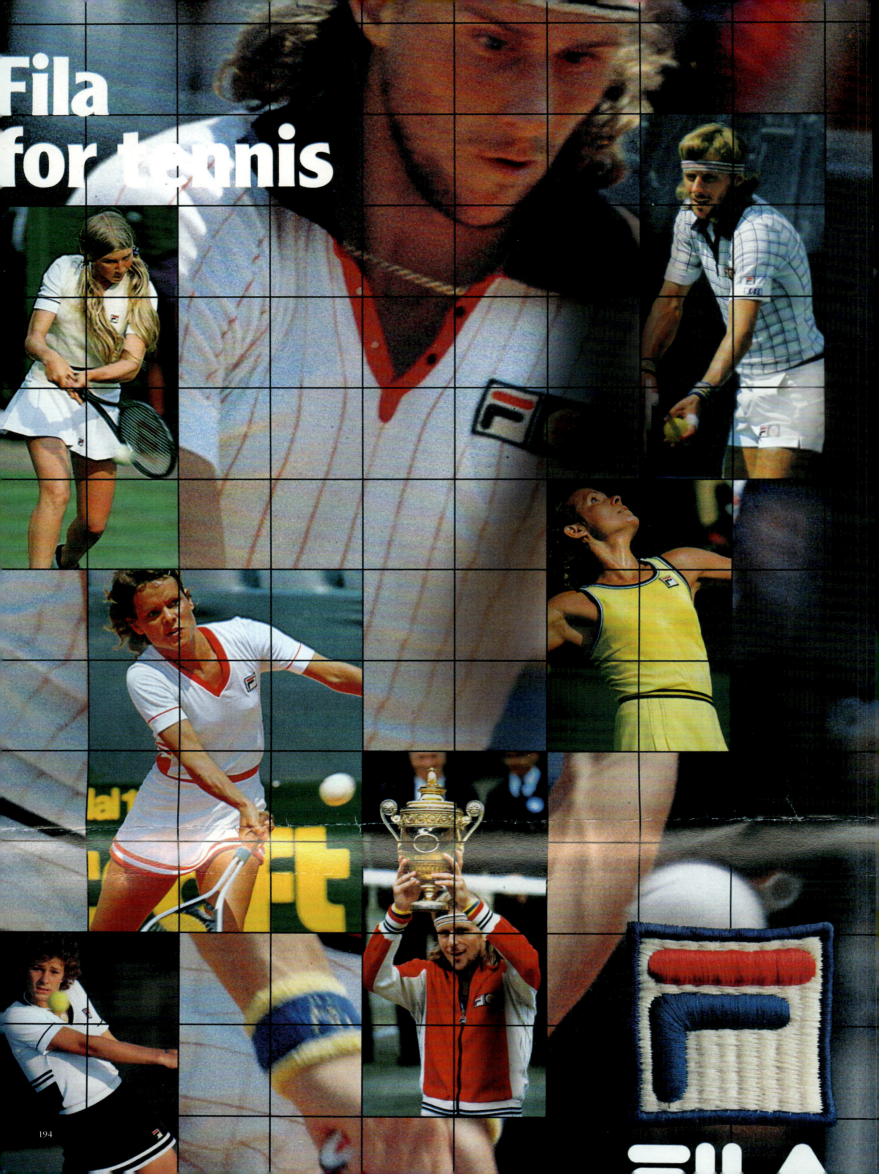

PLAY ITALIAN

F2002 · TEAM REPLICA COLLECTION

has taken the latitude to reinvent your irons.

We outdistance the field. Superior performance across the board.

Webster defines Lat•i•tude — as freedom of action, choice and form.

MESSNER e FILA
Restano solo 4 "ottomila" da scalare.

LHOTSE m. 8501

MAKALU m. 8481

DHAULAGIRI m. 8167

ANNAPURNA m. 8091

Per lui, non c'è l'impossibile. Nemmeno scalare l'Everest senza bombole d'ossigeno. Amore per la montagna, scientifica preparazione atletica, un fisico eccezionale: ecco Messner! Che indossa durante le sue leggendarie imprese capi Fila: per la completa libertà dei movimenti, la perfetta protezione termica, la resistenza a tutta prova nelle più avverse condizioni ambientali e climatiche. Fila e Messner: una collaborazione che ha fatto fare passi da gigante ai capi tecnici per la montagna. A beneficio di tutti gli sportivi.

4 Wimbledon: 4 Borg!

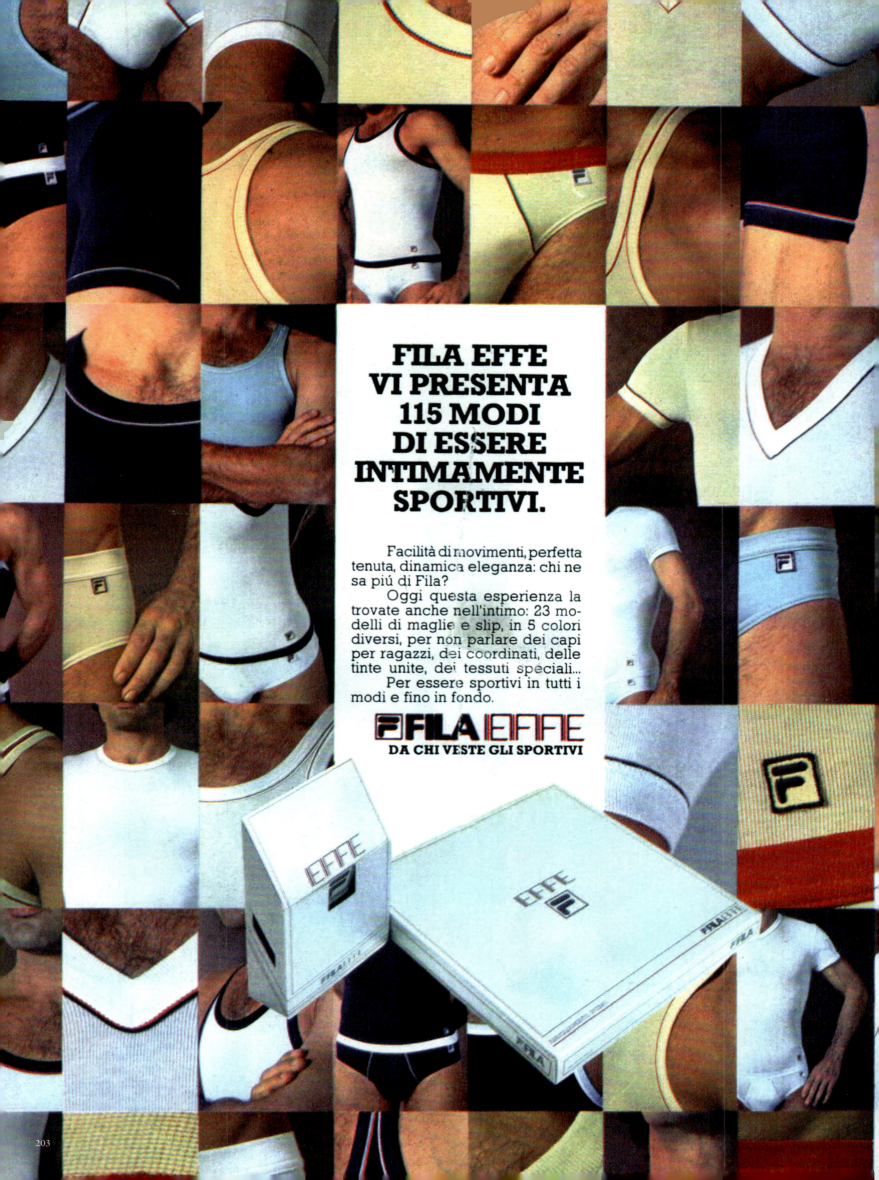

LINE FILA
Rod LEVER

WHITE

linea PANATTA

KINGDOM OF DREAMS
Rahim Attarzadeh

Even dreams live on a budget in Soviet Russia. In a 1984 chronicle of Moscow lay the most industrious dereliction of what the city was, what it had been, and what it went on to become. Dreams have a spectacular imagination about how to make ends meet. In this kingdom of dreams, it weeds out the weak preying on the city's individuals who dare to dream: people high on determination who can only afford to luxuriate into the future, eradicating any desire for nostalgia.

Most dreams didn't make it to reality here. Under the KGB's watchful eye in the 1980s, death lurked in Moscow's underground, the lungs of the city. The Soviet Union kept all foreigners segregated from the Russians —deepening and widening death by numbers to the death of culture. Mostly on the yellow, orange, green, and white metro lines. Rarely red, even less than that blue— the retrograde colors of FILA. Such decay bumps up against the city's ambitions, its determinations, at the time mostly on spooky-eyed transplants—the blue-collared backdrop of the government's appetite for industrialization. Block after block, the proletariats stared aimlessly biting at the nails of their dreams, hoping to catch a break, spitting their remains out through the factories fumes and all over the city like pennies tossed in a wishing fountain. They yearned for a radical reorganization of society. "Reorganization" being an anodyne term for cultural revolution.

However, revolution doesn't always work out this way.

Meanwhile, in what seemed like a sequestered land in New York, death crossed paths with dream catchers, rebel threaders, disc jockeys, fashion designers, and downtown dwellers. These practically chimerical figures only appeared transcendental in trajectory and notoriety compared to those living under the autocracy of Soviet Russian rule.

Death doesn't stop at trajectory; death doesn't halt at accolades. The AIDS epidemic in New York saw death stomp on accolades and crush such trajectories. On a blue line, the C train most likely. Death was ready to catch its prey but the city was too distracted to see death coming, too possessed by idols framed on bedroom walls. Stop after stop death looked on, as the likes of Grandmaster Flash coolly scratched Donna Summer's *Last Dance*—an allegory for New York City's "last dance" as it fought for survival.

Above ground, death can spread into the guts of subculture, infecting the pages of history books and the social life of dreams. Dance floors and B-boys took center stage, sporting FILA jumpsuits, windbreakers, bucket hats, and T1 mid-leather sneakers, colored with creative impulses you thought might last forever, that might seek eternity. Only to fade away as death approached. The next you-know-who and you-know-what vanish at the moment the DJ goes on to spin Shannon's *Let the Music Play*, looking death in the eye and blinking. By the time the DJ opened his eyes, that very same scene became a Westernized utopia of propaganda. An injection of capital to whitewash the history books. Not cathartic but rather chaotic. A new fast-food joint or a shopping center. Where murky memories became muddied on sticky bathroom walls, dancing like phantom limbs.

Sending memories into oblivion every time you walked by. As fast as it is to switch a record, the history books move on to a new chapter.

Scratch, flip, and turn the page. The MC calls for capitalism.

The USSR was on the verge of collapse by 1991. Calls, cries, and begging for radical reform to introduce capitalism into the crux of society came rippling through Russia's smokestack surface. Its citizens wanted to smile, to laugh; they wanted to live the allure of democratic freedom. Allure doesn't stand too far away from dreams. The American fast-food phenomenon McDonald's finally opened its doors to Russia in the 1990s.

Execrable trains muscled through rat-infested tunnels reeking of piss and shit. Whole cars were vandalized end-to-end, front-to-back, and inside-and-out. Subway lights flickered on and off, sprawling on wheels that squealed like spellbinding chills down your spine. Moscow's nine-to-fivers took their chances elsewhere, leaving the subway to thick-accented "Lemme get a double bacon cheeseburger" city dwellers lining up at the red and yellow hues of hope that signaled McDonald's.

"Opening its doors" was the emblem that faked its way through Russia's newfound state of ambition as it attempted to put death in the rearview mirror. Only for allure to settle in and infect and affect any configuration of hope. Many dreamed that the fall of the Soviet Union meant that Western goods would become available. That Nick Kamen's Levi's 501 ad in 1985 would soon become a palpable reality to those now forced to live and forced to stay in Russia. Only for reality to reveal the misfortunes of tragedy and tribulation—that money had no value. Hyperinflation surmounted any aesthetic dreams and sensibilities Moscow's citizens yearned for. The West seemed as far away as ever. This time, though, they knew what they were dreaming for: beacons of quality and avatars of hope that would fuel the democratization of cults, or just offer a pocket of culture. Levi's and McDonald's—or just *McCool*.

Even the city's politicians didn't adjourn their daily meetings at the mere obstacle of hyperinflation. The city began building its concrete plans for what President Boris Yeltsin called "public cultural institutions" and visceral desires for congregation; but this kingdom of dreams was already built on cracked foundations. Russia refused to be victimized by the West. The shifting geopolitics in Russia began meeting its peripheral Western-occupied domains throughout the 1990s. For the first time allowing multiple visions and interpretations, mobilizing what was once an immobile city forced to live through an induced coma of cultural isolation. A dawn of a new era and of new creativity could be harnessed through education centers such as the Moscow College of Technology and Design, ravaging the communist belly of the USSR beast.

Dreams brushed shoulders with its alumni—Gosha Rubchinskiy.

Only, he was able to catch them. Most likely while sweating it out on a dance floor at Fontanka River, No. 145's appetite for hysteric glamour in 1990s underground Russia with the likes of youth and pop culture agent provocateurs, DJ Zhit Vredno and Pavel Milyukov, the artist otherwise known as Buttechno. Moscow's dance scene in the 1990s—a more emulsified continuation of its late 1980s precursor—was the most earnest lung of the city. The rise of the St. Petersburg rave was born. Moscow's nighttime heroes looked strikingly different from the Soviet public outside, with rings in ears and noses, dyed and spiked hair, and unusual and colorful clothes, painting a great potential for experimentation and learning—"Anarchy in the USSR." The relentless attacks on political identity, ideology, and state institutions of power reached their zenith. Moscow's citizens needed a release. Out of great necessity, great creativity was born, although through a context materialized by death, dreams, and desperation. For Moscow and its creative scene, iconography could only be iconized through such destruction and through the formation of a new breeding ground, of a new society incited by chaos and despair.

Moscow was headed toward bankruptcy. Rents were barely affordable above and below the Kremlin. A diverse community of artists forged a radically experimental counterculture. The likes of Rubchinskiy were shaken by Russia's rejection of culture and invigorated by the energy pulsating through the capital, the womb that birthed the golden age of Russian nightlife and culture. Rubchinskiy's dreams provided unique material and context for his symbolic creativity that segued to the emergence of a new wave of youth subculture organized by a troop of unofficial artists, musicians, and friends in St. Petersburg. Together they produced all-night dance parties—ending the Soviet era, ultimately spreading to the rest of St. Petersburg, to Moscow, and then to other neighboring cities. Blood, sweat, and tears birthed Rubchinskiy's creative impulses.

Rubchinskiy had dreams and death on his mind too. He couldn't ignore such obstacles because he grew up with this all around him, in him even. Not just death by statistics. He was fearless as he never stopped dreaming, even after seeing those held at gunpoint for carrying the same dreams. With his fuse-wire physique and all that anger at his own nation bubbling like foam erupting from his scalp, it didn't seem as if there was much more to him than essence; as if his whole personality had been distilled from an inflammable creative drive. In an atmosphere where Moscow's social infrastructure was being dismantled, Rubchinskiy yearned for and constructed an alternative point of view, coming loose at the seams with cracks and vacancies. Post-Soviet nihilism riddled his Western desires and predilections in a space suspended outside the institutional state power; an ideal place for new creative experiments.

Through the red, blue, and white undertones of FILA, Rubchinskiy's designs would birth his own kingdom of dreams, evaded by the ghosts of Moscow's Soviet past.

Like negotiating with anger, Rubchinskiy sketched a structural complexity that distorted its narrative clarity from his small bedroom in Moscow. Suspending time and space, the braided stripes of a FILA sweatshirt broke the confines of Soviet Russia's ball and chain, adorned by Rubchinskiy's New York City record collection. It wasn't easy to imagine him boiling an egg without it being part of some ingenious agenda. Rubchinskiy had such an ingenious thirst for attention and information because of an innate desire to escape death and enter a faraway Western land he and his comrades dreamed of inhabiting. Every action was a project to which he would commit his last subversive molecule, for Rubchinskiy was a figure made entirely out of counterculture. Someone who had flared inevitably into being from Russia's tinder times, a petrol spirit without permeable or precedent.

The colors of FILA pre-empted the selective political nostalgia fortifying Rubchinskiy's creative output; as much as he and his friends campaigned against it. They chanted for the likes of Gorbachev in the street. They waved the flags of emancipation and a move away from the mad, oppressing, Soviet, Gotham-like world they were born in, constrained by the weight of all-too-powerful and greedy politicians hoarding America's freedoms. A memory zooms in on a young man sitting on the floor of his bedroom, knees folded to his chest. He's wearing a FILA sweatshirt with blue denim Levi's jeans and his hair is shaved, whose thorough excavations finally expose his narrative along with the pre-torn and slogan-stenciled fabric of his youth.

What Rubchinskiy didn't know then is what he may know now.

There couldn't be Soviet culture at all without dreams. There couldn't be symbols of creativity and out of their new place, an anti-Soviet criticism. There couldn't be new "symbolic samples," containing quotes from past and recent Soviet meanings that were placed into a dynamic new cultural context. Those who dared to dream, those who dared to fight death, and those who pursued a creative life, not spreading their hopes and ambitions across Moscow's factory floors, gambled on an end to industrialization with a new lease of life. A life known in the in-between, like toes dangling from a cliff of acceptance and on the edge of a come up. Like, "it was all a dream," only Rubchinskiy's eyes were never closed. He lived for his dreams to reclaim his own individuality. He had to become more than a fashion designer. He had to become a world builder and decorate it with color and hope. In this world, like he appears in this text, he always saw his clothes as one part of a larger story. Of one nation's road away from perdition. This prolific artistic experiment helped Rubchinskiy's journey with a dissenting voice that pushed back against a nation of domination, the censorship of humanity, egalitarianism, individualism, and imagination.

In Rubchinskiy's kingdom of dreams, hope returns to its rightful place at the center of his life. The ghosts of death that haunted his youth have no bearing upon time, present or future, because living under such oppression means the world can be taken from you any day, therefore every day the world is born anew.

and parcel of their identity, one example being the Fila Fresh Crew—a short-lived trio that appeared in the cult collection *N.W.A. and the Posse* (1987).

Many years before, FILA had intuited the sales potential of the sporty maverick, the wild superstar, as much a sports icon as a countercultural one, who would never look bad holding an electric guitar instead of a tennis racket. Borg and Panatta had been depicted, first of all by FILA's communications strategy, as two talented and errant playboys. So it should come as no surprise that when the brand opened up to the NBA in 1990, it did so with Grant Hill, a rising star on the Detroit Pistons, also known, because of the way they behaved on the court, as the Bad Boys.

Then a picture of 2Pac with the FILA Grant Hill 1 model did the rest, taking the Piedmontese brand to the United States where, in 1993, it was floated on the New York Stock Exchange, becoming the world's number-three sneaker along with Nike and Reebok. FILA planned advertising campaigns, such as the one for FX100 footwear, on urban playgrounds, that underscored the seamless link between sportswear and streetwear, between the parquet floor and concrete, between the stars of the NBA and the kids on the street.

FILA clothing, which had become baggy and came in neon colors, was now popular on the dance floors and warehouses of Europe because of its ability to combine comfort and design. The Gabbers, albeit not turning the brand into one of their style mainstays, used it off and on. Once again, FILA became at the same time an unexpected protagonist of the underground and pop culture. The Disruptors, very popular with clubbers, were meant to be a cross-training type of footwear, originally exclusive to the German market, before experiencing a successful comeback in recent years. At the same time, FILA was the gray sweatshirt brand worn by Britney Spears when, in 2007, she showed up at a hairdresser's in Los Angeles asking them to shave off all her hair.

So FILA was not just a tennis and sneaker brand that left a countercultural imprint. The editorial "Trekking in Nepal" (*Fila* no. 2, 1976) seemed to recount a proto-Gorpcore philosophy that, ten years later, would become part of the experiments conducted by Nike AGC, Patagonia, and Arc'teryx.

In soccer, where the liaison between Rolando's designs and the youth culture had blossomed, FILA went from the terraces to the field when, in the 1990s, it produced a series of kits that symbolically appeared to close this circle. Most importantly, the one for West Ham United (1999–2001), whose commercial sponsor Dr. Martens seemed to harken back to the working-class origins of the East End and the Skinhead scene. Acting as a catalyst for this narrative was Paolo Di Canio, who, with his rude boy look and volley goal against Wimbledon entered the history of the London-based club.

And so, over the decades, FILA has been able to build up a considerable subcultural legacy that, during a period of the rediscovery of the theme of the archive, has contributed to the contemporary rebirth of the brand via situations stemming from that very same street culture. So many streets have been traveled down, for a brand that started out as clothes for clay court tennis fans.

FOOTWEAR 2000
Fall & Winter

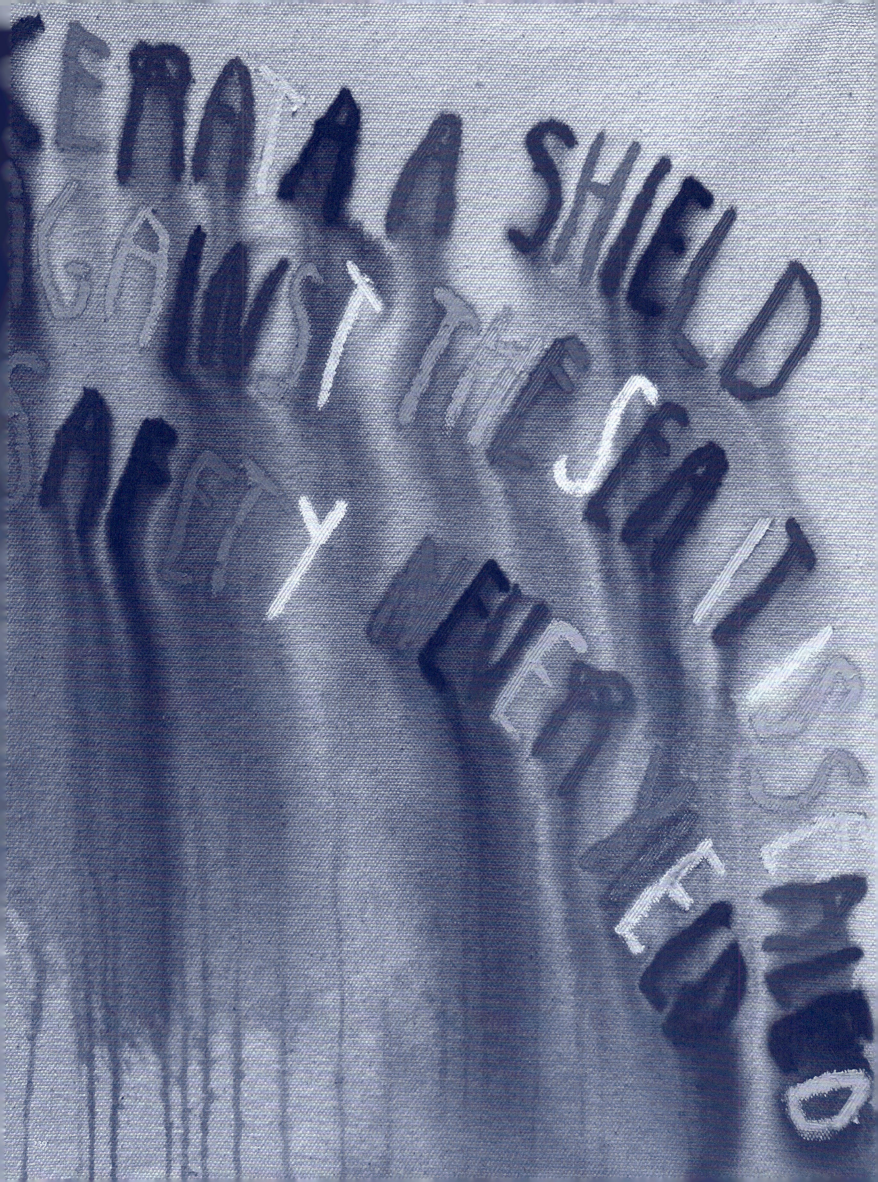

FILA: INSIDE AND OUTSIDE FASHION
Angelo Flaccavento

Fashion and sports share a strong mutual attraction. Over the decades, sportswear has always reflected the dominant taste and styles—suffice it to recall the simplicity of tennis outfits in the 1970s. The real revolution of the final years of the twentieth century, however, went in the opposite direction: the adoption of sportswear in everyday attire, the predominance of comfort over formality. FILA experienced this movement as a key player, having promptly offered, if not actually invented, garments filled with life and color, which from the tennis court migrated to the wardrobes of the non-sports-playing public. But if we look at designer fashion, at the work of the designers, the phenomenon assumes other features as well. Because it is linked to performance, to the reality of physical activity, sportswear has given fashion myriad ideas and technical solutions—the Chanel jersey, for example—but also a repertoire of clothes to approach and perhaps even revolutionize. This synergy, made up of homages and loans, was for a long time looked upon from a distance, with curiosity and interest, from opposite shores. Then, in 2003, the launch of the Y-3, the union between the authorship of Yohji Yamamoto and the technology of Adidas, changed the course of events. From there a path was launched that burst onto the scene in the 2010s, in a particularly fertile general context that saw a substantial change in shared clothing mores, and a reversal of fates that—with the help of Demna, first with Vetements then with Balenciaga—brought the energy but also the elementariness of streetwear—where sportswear, indeed, dominated—on the catwalks and inside the wardrobes of the new big spenders. In this time lapse and within this context, a productive dialogue opened up between fashion and sports, which breathed life into many forms of collaboration.

Once again FILA played an important role in this phenomenon—a role that initially was not active, but that gradually became so, leading in the end to a genetic mutation whose effects persist to this day. By non-active role we mean the fact that the interconnections between FILA and fashion were not actively searched for in an attempt for the company to reposition itself; quite the contrary, they were instigated from the outside, by authors attracted to the brand's well-established appeal. Unsurprisingly, the first of these was Gosha Rubchinskiy, an agitator of iconographies and the leader of the Sovietization of street aesthetics, which reached a peak halfway through the 2010s. It was June 2016: during Pitti Uomo, in the Brutalist spaces, worthy of the Iron Curtain, of the ex tobacco-making plant in Florence, Rubchinskiy presented the S/S 17 collection, a rough-n'-ready tribute to Pasolinian youths expressed in a combination of dry formality and vintage athleticism. Among the garments, characterized by a tense and aphasic language that for a short period of time turned Rubchinskiy into a phenomenon, were several sportswear items of Italian provenance: Kappa shorts and tank tops, Sergio Tacchini tracksuits, FILA sweatshirts and hoodies in their unmistakable white-red-blue triad of hues, and the F-Box logo accompanied by the second logo, Gosha Rubchinskiy, written out in Cyrillic. This short passage was like the shock of a defibrillator: *ipso facto* it put the FILA imaginary back into play, re-awakening memories and affiliations that at that moment in time, it has to be said, were dormant. What made these pieces particularly special was the allure of counterfeit copies, the appearance of designer fakes. Far from being a real design operation, Gosha's together with FILA was substantially an experiment in subcultural repositioning, one that was particularly effective because the link between FILA and the youth cultures has always been strong.

The real change for FILA and the trendsetters arrived two years later, with Fendi's F/W 18–19 collection, presented in Milan in February 2018. The chronology, in this genetic mutation, is important, because every stage contributed to shaping FILA's process and new identity. Following the order of the facts helps, if not to decode them entirely, at least to contextualize them. In Fendi's case, the encounter was triggered by the digital artist Hey Reilly, a skilled manipulator of the signs of popular culture. As part of the Instagram series *#fakenews*, Hey Reilly had already mixed up the Fendi and FILA logos, recomposing the word FENDI ROMA in FILA's classic F-Box font: an action that drew the attention of Silvia Venturini Fendi, who turned it into a product labeled Fendi, thus validating from above, with a touch of irony, the practice known as "brandalism," that is, the vandalism of the brand. The capsule collection that was the fruit of this joint project was given the name Fendi Mania, and it was characterized, once again, by the appearance of designer fakes, contradicted, however, by Fendi's very *haute* craftsmanship: F-Box logos knitted onto mink sweaters, or repeated in a jacquard and fil coupé pattern on dresses, blouses, and skirts of doubtless bon ton. Brought inside the system of an upper-middle-class wardrobe, the name FILA underwent an unexpected semantic shift, revealing potentials in fields very distant from the original ones, taking advantage of the viral nature and immediacy of Instagram culture.

Along its pathway inside and outside of fashion, FILA experienced, in tune with the fashion of the moment, a constant tension between street style and actual design. A fundamental difference in this sense was the collaboration with the stylist, creative director, and cultural curator Katie Grand in 2021, when the brand held a multichannel celebration of its 110th anniversary. From that moment onward, conversations aimed at fashion enthusiasts would actively be sought after by FILA. The aim, in terms of marketing strategy, was that of re-evaluating and re-affirming the company's heritage by dovetailing in an active and purposeful way with the growing wave of designer sportswear.

The 110th Anniversary Collection thus celebrates FILA's heritage thanks to the curatorship of a particularly well-known and influential publisher, synergistically tied to contemporary pop culture. The choice of an editor, instead of a designer, is significant, as well as being appropriate: it is indeed via the rebellious act of daily self-styling that sportswear permanently entered the metropolitan style, well before being embraced by the designers. Grand realized for FILA an operation based on selection and new editions, one that was aimed at the assemblage so as to make the meanings of style burst forth, and focused on themes like tennis, the mountains, water, aerobics, basketball, golf, and motorsports to underscore FILA's identifying features. The pieces she selected, chosen based on historical and aesthetic value, were reproposed as anastatic copies, only partially redesigned, therefore maintaining the vintage allure that is an assurance of beauty and authenticity. Although it was presented as a curatorial work, the project actively brought the fashion mentality inside FILA, definitively paving the way for formal experimentation that would soon be manifested.

Again in 2021, and then as part of the 110th anniversary, FILA worked with a particularly radical talent: Glenn Martens, creative director, from 2013, of the Parisian brand Y/PROJECT. The choice of this sparring partner, someone with a vision of design that is both complex and playful, in which hypermasculine and hyperfeminine merge in a multifarious and allencompassing identity, appears to be timely and appropriate, and filled with a feeling of competitive daring. Martens's fashion is not easy; rather, it is challenging, at times confusing, because it is based on an anamorphic distortion of the structures, and on the idea that the forms of each single piece of clothing can be shaped endlessly. A creator who is inclined toward the hybrid, Martens approaches FILA by focusing on a series of basic pieces —the T-shirt, the hoodie, the dress, the polo shirt, and the windbreaker—and then distorts them with structural details that are also an invitation, for the wearer, to use them inventively: double necklines and round necks, multiplying snap buttons, asymmetrical closings, Siamese T-shirts. In Martens's vision, which is heterodoxical by definition, there are no univocal rules: everything goes and personal interpretations are welcome. With this collaboration, FILA embraced daring experimentation, but while remaining fresh, because the work of alteration maintained the recognizability of the pieces. The result was a language that was comprehensible but bewildering, familiar but not entirely so.

Along FILA's fashion journey, the following collaboration, in March 2022 for the F/W 22–23 collection, with Roksanda, full name Roksanda Ilinčić, instead represented a moment of movement toward far-flung territories, of inventive but no less evident lady-like style. Ilinčić, who received a degree from Central Saint Martins in London after training in Architecture and the Applied Arts in her native Belgrade, found a space in the system that is entirely hers, forging a language in the exorbitant volumes and off colors put together idiosyncratically to create a sophisticated and expressive vocabulary. Sports are in no way a part of her language. Hence, for the collaboration her dramatic shapes and bright colors meet FILA's technical side, breathing life into protective down jackets with long ribbons to fasten them, windbreakers, and oversized moonboots as accessories. The gigantification is also a chromatic affair here: gone is the blue, the white, the red, in favor of a tropical mix of porcelain, black, and neon orange with notes of chalk, champagne, butter, pearl, dove, and neon pink. Everything that isn't FILA, but that is still perfectly FILA, with the logo on top to seal it all.

FILA's encounter with Roksanda represents, in many ways, the company's extreme attempt to emerge from its comfort zone, and it was followed by the collaboration with Haider Ackermann on an entire collection for the S/S 23 season. This opus, an accomplished and articulated one, deserved, unlike previous collaborations that were seen on the catwalks in small doses, an entire fashion show all to itself, outside the calendar, in a place chosen specially for it—Manchester. Ackermann, like Ilinčić, might at first be viewed as an unwise match, perhaps even a mad one: a creator who is too rarefied and elitist, on paper, to embrace the sports ethos of FILA. And instead, the combination was perfect: tense, electric, veiled with nostalgia mixed with high-performance technology, and set in a run-down warehouse that amplified the acceleration of saturated and acidic colors, worthy of a rave party.

Doing a fashion show is the equivalent of trendsetting imprinting, it admits one into the Gotha of the system. By doing a show, FILA sanctions the definitive creation of a hybrid language between fashion and sports, technical in terms of its use, sophisticated in terms of its forms. In Haider Ackermann's collection for FILA what stands out are the clean lines, the energy of the color, which is saturated and like signage, the physicality that is tense and present and accentuated by the materials. This encounter is thus the last step along the way, but also the start of what comes after. From that moment onward FILA changes again, it freezes the strategy of the collaborations—whose trajectory is declining, broadly speaking, in the territories of fashion—but it introjects the signs and the ideas accumulated over these past years. A sign of this can instantly be seen in the first Global collection: just perceptible but clear in the definition of the details, in the study of the volumes, in the use of colors and materials. The evolution of the species is in full swing. The DNA is there, unchanged, but there is an extra filament interwoven with that base, which keeps FILA together, inside fashion, and yet solidly outside, too, on a path that is all its own. Leaving mores aside, today FILA is a sportswear brand that creates fashion.

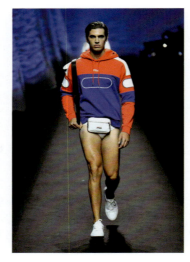

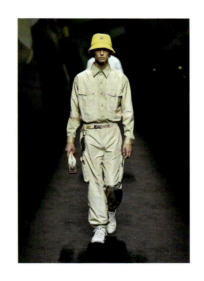

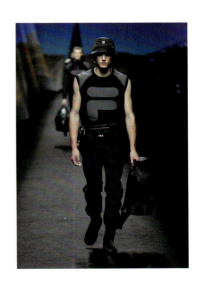

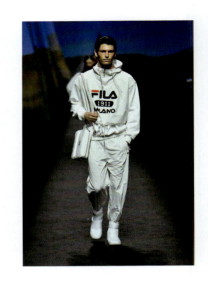

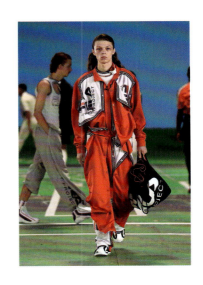

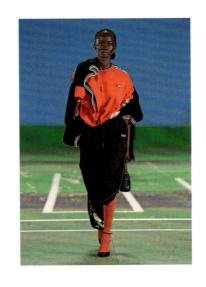

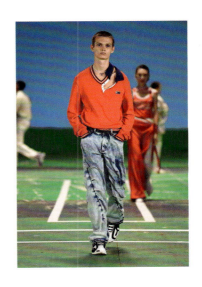

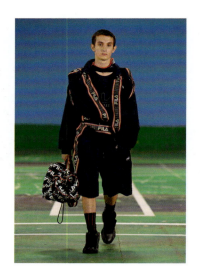

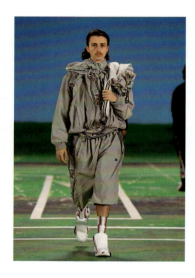

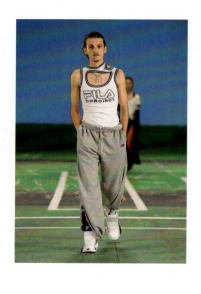

20–21 ➡️➡️
Underwear collection catalogue, Italy, 1973.
"White Line" collection, Italian sales catalogue, 1982.
"White Line" collection, tennis photo shoot, circa 1975.

22–23 ➡️➡️
"White Line" collection, tennis photo shoot, circa 1975.
"FILA for Mountain" collection, photo shoot, 1981.
Golf collection, Winter 1982, Italian sales catalogue.

24–25 ➡️➡️
Golf collection, Winter 1982, Italian sales catalogue.
Underwear collection catalogue, Italy, 1973.
"FILA for Skiing" collection, F/W 1982, Italian sales catalogue.

26–27 ➡️➡️
"FILA for Skiing" collection, F/W 1982, Italian sales catalogue.
"Aqua Time" collection, 1982, Italian sales catalogue, technical sheet.
Golf collection, Winter 1982, Italian sales catalogue.

28–29 ➡️➡️
Golf collection, Winter 1982, Italian sales catalogue.
"FILA for Swimming" collection, Italian sales catalogue.
"Aqua Time" collection, 1979, French catalogue.

30–31 ➡️➡️
"Aqua Time" collection, 1979, French catalogue.

"White Rock" collection, Winter 1981, Italian sales catalogue.
"White Line" collection, 1974, sketches by Pierluigi Rolando.

32–33 ➡️➡️
"White Line" collection, 1974, sketches by Pierluigi Rolando.
"White Line" collection, 1982, Italian sales catalogue.
Underwear collection catalogue, Italy, 1973.

34–35 ➡️➡️
Underwear collection catalogue, Italy, 1973.
"Snow Time" collection, F/W 1989, Italian sales catalogue.

"White Rock" collection, Winter 1982, Italian sales catalogue, technical sheet.

36–37 ➡️➡️
"White Rock" collection, Winter 1982, Italian sales catalogue, technical sheet.
"Aqua Time" collection, 1979, French catalogue.
Golf collection, Winter 1982, Italian sales catalogue.

38–39 ➡️➡️
Golf collection, Winter 1982, Italian sales catalogue.
Underwear collection catalogue, Italy, 1973.
"Snow Time" collection, F/W 1989, Italian sales catalogue.

40–41 ➡️➡️
"Snow Time" collection, F/W 1989, Italian sales catalogue.

"White Rock" collection, S/S 1977, sketches by Pierluigi Rolando.

Sailing collection, 1983, Italian sales catalogue.

42–43 ➡️➡️
Sailing collection, 1983, Italian sales catalogue.
"White Line" collection, F/W 1989, Italian sales catalogue.
"White Line" collection, circa 1975, photo shoot.

44–45 ➡️➡️
"White Line" collection, circa 1975, photo shoot.
"FILA for Mountain" collection 1981, photo shoot.
"Aqua Time" collection, 1979, French catalogue.

46–47 ➡️➡️
"Aqua Time" collection, 1979, French catalogue.
"White Line" collection, 1982, Italian sales catalogue, technical sheet.
Underwear collection catalogue, Italy, 1973.

48 ⬅️➡️
Underwear collection catalogue, Italy, 1973.
"White Line" collection, S/S 1985, Italian sales catalogue.

53 🔘
"Aqua Time" collection, S/S 1984, Italian sales catalogue.

53 ↗️↙️↘️
"Aqua Time" collection, S/S 1984, still life, Italian sales catalogue.

54 ↖
"Aqua Time" collection, S/S 1984, Italian sales catalogue.

54 ↗↙↘
"Aqua Time" collection, S/S 1984, still life, Italian sales catalogue.

55 ↖

"Aqua Time" collection, S/S 1984, Italian sales catalogue.

55 ↗↙↘
"Aqua Time" collection, S/S 1984, still life, Italian sales catalogue.

56
"Aqua Time" collection, S/S 1984, CAD, Italian sales catalogue

57
"Aqua Time" collection, S/S 1984, Italian sales catalogue.

58 ↖
"Aqua Time" collection, S/S 1984, Italian sales catalogue.

58 ↗↙↘
"Aqua Time" collection, S/S 1984, still life, Italian sales catalogue.

59

"Aqua Time" collection, S/S 1984, Italian sales catalogue.

60
"Aqua Time" collection, S/S 1984, Italian sales catalogue.

63
"White Line" collection, 1984, Italian sales catalogue.

64
"White Line" collection, 1982, Italian sales catalogue.

65
"White Line" collection, 1983, Italian sales catalogue.

66
"White Line" collection, 1982, Italian sales catalogue.

67 ↖↙

"White Line" collection, 1982, Borg Line, Italian sales catalogue.

67 ↗↘
"White Line" collection, 1982, Italian sales catalogue.

68
"White Line" collection, 1984, Italian sales catalogue.

69
"White Line" collection, 1984, Italian sales catalogue.

70
"White Line" collection, 1984, Italian sales catalogue.

71
"White Line" collection, 1984, Italian sales catalogue.

72
"White Line" collection, circa 1975, photo shoot.

73
"White Line" collection, circa 1975, photo shoot.

74 ↖
"White Line" collection, F/W 1989, Italian sales catalogue.

74 ↗↙

"White Line" collection, 1982, Italian sales catalogue.

74 ↘
"White Line" collection, 1983, Italian sales catalogue.

75 ↖↗
"White Line" collection, F/W 1986, Italian sales catalogue.
"White Line" collection, 1989, Italian sales catalogue.

75 ↙↘
"White Line" collection, 1983, Italian sales catalogue.

76
"White Line" collection, 1983, Italian sales catalogue.

77
"White Line" collection, F/W 1986, Italian sales catalogue.

78
"White Line" collection, S/S 1987, Italian sales catalogue.

79
"White Line" accessories collection, 1983, Italian sales catalogue.

80
"White Line" collection, S/S 1990, Italian sales catalogue.

81
"White Line" collection, S/S 1990, Italian sales catalogue.

82 ↙↘
"White Line" collection, 1983, Italian sales catalogue.

82 ↗↙

"White Line" collection, 1984, Italian sales catalogue.

83 ↖↗↙
"White Line" collection, 1983, Italian sales catalogue.

83 ↘
"White Line" collection, S/S 1985, Italian sales catalogue.

84
"White Line" collection, S/S 1990, Italian sales catalogue.

85
"White Line" collection, S/S 1990, Italian sales catalogue.

86 ↖↗↘
"White Line" collection, F/W 1990, Italian sales catalogue.

86 ↙
"White Line" collection, S/S 1990, Italian sales catalogue.

87 ↖↗
"White Line" collection, S/S 1989, Italian sales catalogue.

87 ↙↘
"White Line" collection, S/S 1987, Italian sales catalogue.

88
"White Line" collection, S/S 1990, Italian sales catalogue.

89
"White Line" collection, S/S 1990, Italian sales catalogue.

90
"White Line" accessories collection, 1984, Italian sales catalogue.

91 ↖↗
"White Line" collection, S/S 1987, Italian sales catalogue.

91 ↙↘
"White Line" collection, F/W 1990, Italian sales catalogue.

92
"White Line" collection, F/W 1986, Italian sales catalogue.

97
Björn Borg, WCT Tournament, Mexico City, 1976.

98
Björn Borg, Roland Garros Tournament, Paris, 1979.

99
Björn Borg, Internazionali d'Italia Tournament, Rome, 1978.

100
Björn Borg, US Open, New York, 1977.

101
Björn Borg, Tennis collection, photo shoot, Monte Carlo, 1977.

102
Björn Borg, Monte Carlo Masters, Monte Carlo, 1981.

103
Björn Borg, Monte Carlo Masters, Monte Carlo, 1982.

104
Björn Borg, US Open, New York, 1978.

107
Alberto Tomba, Nagano Winter Olympics, 1998.

108 ↖↗↙↘
Reinhold Messner, Nanga Parbat expedition, Pakistan, 1978.
Reinhold Messner, Broad Peak expedition, China/Pakistan, 1979.
Reinhold Messner training, Italy, 1978.
Reinhold Messner and Hans Kammerlander, Makalu expedition, China/Nepal, 1986.

109 ↖↗↙↘
Giorgio Bertone, Courmayeur, 1975.
Giorgio Bertone, Mountain collection, Grandes Jorasses, 1976.
Yannick Seigneur, 1977.
Renzino Cosson, El Capitan expedition, Yosemite Park, 1974.

110
Reinhold Messner, Antarctic expedition, 1989.

111
Alberto Tomba,
Vail, 1996.

112
Grant Hill, Basket
collection photo shoot,
Milano Tour 1998.

113
Jerry Stackhouse,
"Big Gym" event,
Stadio dei Marmi,
Rome, 1998.

113
Jerry Stackhouse, "Change
the Game" advertising
campaign for Stack Mid
shoes, Philadelphia, 1997.

114
Gabriela Sabatini, photo
shoot, New York,
1996.

115
Monica Seles, Wimbledon
Tournament, Wimbledon,
London, 1989.

115
Monica Seles, Roland
Garros Tournament, Paris,
1989.

Monica Seles,
Roland Garros
Tournament,
Paris 1990.

116
Björn Borg, Tennis
collection photo shoot,
Monte Carlo, 1981.

117
Björn Borg, Tennis
collection photo shoot,
Monte Carlo, 1977.

118
"White Line," S/S 1990,
Monica Seles collection,
Italian sales catalogue.

119
Monica Seles, Key Biscayne
Tournament, Florida, 1991.

120
Jennifer Capriati, Australian Open Tournament,
Melbourne Park, Victoria,
Australia, 2002.

121
Andrea Jaeger, US Open,
USA, 1980.

122
Jennifer Capriati, WTA
Tournament, Los Angeles,
2002.

123
Boris Becker,
Monte Carlo
Masters, Monte
Carlo, 1991.

124
Boris Becker, ATP Nabisco
Masters finals, New York,
1989.

125
Evonne Goolagong Cawley,
Wimbledon photo shoot,
Wimbledon, London, 1977.
Evonne Goolagong
Cawley, US Open Tennis
Championship, New York,
1979.

125
Evonne Goolagong
Cawley, Tennis
collection photo
shoot, 1978.

126
Adriano Panatta, Davis
Cup, France, 1975.

127
Gianluigi Buffon wearing
a Parma FC uniform,
Stadio Ennio Tardini,
Parma, 1999.

128
Paolo Di Canio wearing
a West Ham United FC
uniform, Boleyn Ground
Stadium, London, 2001.

129
Gabriel Omar Batistuta
wearing an ACF Fiorentina
uniform while playing
against Piacenza Calcio
1919 (Serie A Championship), Artemio Franchi
stadium, Florence, March
4, 2000.

130
Reinhold Messner,
portrait, 1976.

131
Germán Silva, portrait,
1998.

132
Marco Pantani,
Giro d'Italia, 1999.

133
Marco Pantani,
Giro d'Italia, 1999.

134
Germán Silva at the
Vertical Kilometer Open,
Val d'Isère, France, 1997.
Germán Silva at New York
City Marathon, New York,
USA, 1997

134
Germán Silva at New York
City Marathon, New York,
USA, 1994.

135
Kim Clijsters, Australian
Open, Melbourne Park,
Victoria, Australia, 2011.

136
Grant Hill photo shoot, 1998.

141

"Snow Time" collection, F/W 1990, technical sheet, Italian sales catalogue.

142
"Snow Time" collection, F/W 1989, technical sheet, Italian sales catalogue.

143
"Snow Time" collection, F/W 1989, technical sheet, Italian sales catalogue.

144
"Snow Time" collection, F/W 1990, technical sheet, Italian sales catalogue.

145
"Snow Time" collection, F/W 1989, technical sheet, Italian sales catalogue.

146
"Snow Time" collection, F/W 1989, technical sheet, Italian sales catalogue.

147

"Snow Time" collection, F/W 1989, technical sheet, Italian sales catalogue.

148
"Snow Time" collection, F/W 1990, technical sheet, Italian sales catalogue.

151
FILA Linear logo registration trademark, 1979.

152
"White Line" stickers, 1974.

153
"Snow Time" collection, 1978, Italian sales catalogue.

154
Tennis collection, Italian sales catalogue, 2000.

155
"FILA Cycles" collection, 1991, US clothing and accessories collection.

156–157
Template for embroidered logos, 1992.

158
Launch of Lancia Y10 FILA, *The Marque*, 1987.

159
"White Line" collection, stickers, circa 1974.

160
FILA Globe stickers, circa 1969.

161
"FILA for Tennis" international folder, 1982.

162–163
Template for embroidered logos, 1992.

164
"White Line" collection advertising page, 1974.

169
Reinhold Messner, Mount Everest expedition base camp, China/Pakistan, 1980.

170

Reinhold Messner, K2 expedition, China/Pakistan, 1979.

171
Reinhold Messner training, Italy, 1979.

172
Reinhold Messner, photo shoot, 1976.

173
Reinhold Messner, photo shoot, 1979.

174
Reinhold Messner, photo shoot, 1977.

175
Reinhold Messner, photo shoot, 1976.

176
Interview of Reinhold Messner, *FILA Magazine*, 1981.

179
"Change the Game" advertising campaign, S/S 1997, FILA B-Ball Station catalogue, Germany, 1997.

180
"FILA. Parlami di te" advertising campaign, 1984.

181
"Maglierie Maby Cinture Nobelt" advertising page, 1935.

182
"The Allegro" collection, FILA golf, advertising page, 1992.

183
"Change the Game" advertising campaign, S/S 1997, FILA B-Ball Station catalogue, Germany, 1997.

184
Sport.Life advertising campaign, 2000.

185
Sport.Life advertising campaign, 2000.

186
Proposal sketch for the "You're As Good As You" advertising campaign, 1991.

187
"Change the Game" advertising campaign, 1998.

188
"Change the Game" advertising campaign, 1998.

189
"L'arte nello sport" advertising campaign, 2005.

190
"FILA for Tennis" advertising campaign, 1977.

191
"FILA for Skiing" advertising campaign, 1979.

192
Proposal sketch for the "You're As Good As You" advertising campaign, 1991.

193
FILA Golf advertising campaign, 1992.

194
"FILA – La creatività nello sport" advertising campaign, Italy, 1977.

195
"Play Italian" advertising campaign, F/W 2002, Ferrari Replica collection.

196
Sammy Sosa, postcard, 1999.

197
"Panatta Line" advertising campaign, 1974.

198
Golf wear collection for Tom Watson, S/S 1983, international sports catalogue.

199
FILA golf clubs flyer, "Latitude" collection, circa 1992.

200
Reinhold Messner's expedition program, flyer, 1985.

201
"La creatività nello sport" advertising campaign, Italy, 1979.

202
"4 Wimbledon: 4 Borg!" store window sign, 1979.

203
FILA EFFE advertising campaign, Italy, 1979.

204
"Change the Game" advertising campaign, Barricade cross trainer, 1997.

205
"Panatta Line" advertising folder, 1974.

206
1987 America's Cup, Azzurra sticker.

207
"FILA Sportime" campaign, "Aqua Time" watches, 1992.

208

"Work Hard Have Fun" advertising campaign, France, 1999.

213–220
FILA X Gosha Rubchinskiy fashion show, Pitti Immagine Uomo, Florence, 2016.

224
"European Metropolitan" collection, F/W 1997, European catalogue.

225

Street Sport collection, F/W 1994, Japanese catalogue.

225 ➔
Eddie Van Halen, circa 1982.

226
"The FILA On The Street" collection, S/S 1997, Japanese catalogue.

227
Lola Falana.

228
Street Sport, Ski, and Golf collections, F/W 1994, Japanese catalogue.

229
Footwear collection F/W 2000, Japanese catalogue.

230
Brigitte Nielsen, "Aqua Time" collection S/S 1982, catalogue.

231
Doug E. Fresh, *Oh, My God!* album cover, Reality/Fantasy Records, 1986.

232
Stevie Wonder, circa 1981.

232 ⬇
The Notorious B.I.G., 1993.

233
Gorillaz, 2001.

234
"The FILA On The Street" collection, S/S 1997, Japanese catalogue.

235
Dizzy.

236
Beastie Boys on Charles Street, New York, 1986.

241–248
Giovanni Soldini, Around Alone yachting race, 1998.

251–267
Fashion Week, S/S 2019.
Fashion Week, F/W 2020.
Fashion Week, S/S 2020.
Fashion Week – FILA 110th Anniversary Collection, 2021.
Paris Fashion Week, Y/PROJECT x FILA, S/S 2022.
Manchester Fashion Show, Haider Ackermann and FILA, 2023.

➡ Right
⬅ Left
⬆ Top
⬇ Bottom
↗ Top right
↖ Top left
↙ Bottom left
↘ Bottom right
➡➡ Left to right

FILA ICONS
Marta Franceschini

COLLECTING MEMORIES, SPINNING THE FUTURE

All the stories that make up the history of FILA and illuminate its long journey have been protected from the passage of time and are now available in the archive, a precious container of the objects and memories they represent.
The archive is the place where these memories can be touched, where one can perceive the swirling changes, interruptions, moments of smooth sailing, and sudden upheavals; where technological inventions and visual sophistications are studied, starting precisely from the emotions that these inventions and sophistications have produced. After all, what is a polo shirt, a tracksuit, or a pair of shoes if not a tangible and enduring symbol of the constellation of people who have contributed to creating it and making it iconic?

What follows this brief introduction is a summary made of objects that are particularly important for understanding FILA's role in the evolution of the various sports disciplines the brand has contributed to, and above all, in the affirmation of its idols. Sweatshirts, T-shirts, sweaters, tracksuits: illustrated here is not just FILA history intertwined with the history of sport. It is the history of design, which follows and, in some cases, anticipates the changes in society and in people. Finally, it is the history of fashion, written through stylistic inventions that have been—and still are—capable of turning technicalities and functional details into motifs of taste and desire.
The communicative immediacy of a line; the symbolic meaning of a color or the combination of tones that demonstrate an identity; the value of a volume developed in an unexpected material, the result of collaboration with athletes, understanding their need to overcome, each time, their own limits and those of the discipline they perform.

The archive consists of approximately 15,000 items of clothing, 30,000 shoes, as well as countless documents, sketches, designs, images, and publications. An inestimable heritage, the core of the mission of the Fondazione FILA, which preserves the archive to illustrate the past of the brand, its achievements, and the records it broke, giving voice to the objects which, like milestones in a complicated and beautiful journey, describe the values animating those who produce and those who proudly wear FILA to date.

This selection presents a carefully curated set of objects, whose biographies testify to the richness and durability of human relationships, designed, developed, formed, and consolidated through clothes. Material memories of a constellation of affiliations, personalities, and people, who together wrote important chapters of our immediate past, continuing to inspire innovation and creativity.

By becoming part of an archive, the objects transform their own nature and lend themselves, in a vivid and proactive manner, to the imagination of the future. In this sense, the FILA archive is *alive*—not only because it is open to new acquisitions, which, like rare pieces of a puzzle, contribute to clarifying the scenario that the archive reconstructs, and the complex and fascinating history it represents; but also, and above all, because the archive, composed of artifacts whose details conceal and reveal the possible directions that the brand can take in the future without betraying its cultural heritage, acts as a conceptual and creative starting point. Thus, the greatest value of the archive becomes its "futurability," fundamental to spearheading new projects and inspiring collaborations, joyous collisions of identities, with roots firmly planted in that territory where it all began: varied and harsh, local and global, solid and fertile, perfect for cultivating talent and letting it blossom into success.

IMAGE	PAGE(S)	YEAR	PRODUCT	DESIGNER	FEATURES
	–	1981	Aqua Time swimsuit	Pierluigi Rolando	One-piece swimsuit, gray with oblique stripes in black, white, and light blue. The swimsuit is part of the Aqua Time line, launched by FILA in 1976, as the result of the search for captivating shapes and graphics and, above all, of the best materials suitable for swimming competitions. One of the materials is the "egg skin," an elastic and smooth lycra that counteracts the friction of water.
	–	1982	Aqua Time swimsuit	Pierluigi Rolando	One-shoulder white swimsuit with blue and red stripes that unravel from the right shoulder toward the sides and the center. The stripes imitate the waves, and are an intuition that Pierluigi Rolando translated into a dynamic motif, thanks to the collaboration with Carlo Salussoglia. Transfer-printed on the white background, the "waves" characterize the creations of the first Aqua Time line, inspired by the fluidity of the human body and its movements in water.
	–	1989	US Open 1989 Umpire polo shirt	–	Dark blue polo shirt with white and red details that mark the armholes on both sides. At chest height on the left side, the polo shirt features the FILA logo, while on the right is the wording "US Open 1989 Umpire." After years of absence, in the late 1980s FILA returned to the tennis court, focusing not only on the athletes but on the entire competition, and therefore dressing all the professionals involved in the event.
	–	1990	Polo shirt	–	White polo shirt with red and blue graphic motif that unfolds from the center toward the left shoulder. The polo features two logos: F-Box on the left and BB on the right. It is part of the uniform worn by Boris Becker in 1990, during the Wimbledon final played against Stefan Edberg. Becker became the new face of FILA tennis in 1988, the year in which the brand returned to the court, dressing the new champions: Becker and Monica Seles, and then Gabriela Sabatini, Jennifer Capriati, Mark Philippoussis, Thomas Enqvist, and many more.
	97, 99, 194	1976	Polo shirt	Pierluigi Rolando	Polo shirt with white background marked by thin red vertical lines, with blue collar, red piping, and snap buttons. The FILA logo is present on the left sleeve. The polo shirt represents the synthesis between the brand's desire to explore new scenarios—sport and leisure time—and the awareness of the stylistic features of male elegance: the vertical lines are reminiscent of pinstripes and are well suited to the toned body of the athlete the first prototype of this item was designed for: Björn Borg.
	–	1976	Polo shirt	Pierluigi Rolando	Fiery red polo shirt with collar, short sleeves, and fitted waist. The unexpected shade for the tennis court conceals a political stance: the polo shirt was worn by Adriano Panatta and Paolo Bertolucci, members of the Italian team led by Nicola Pietrangeli at the 1976 Davis Cup. Panatta and Bertolucci wore the red polo shirts during the final, played between December, 17 and 19 in Santiago, Chile, as a sign of solidarity with the Chilean population oppressed by Pinochet's dictatorship.
	–	2002	Polo shirt	–	White cotton polo shirt with sides and details in red. At chest height, on the left, the FILA and Ducati logos are positioned side by side, signaling the collaboration between the two Italian brands. The first FILA collection inspired by the world of motorcycling dates back to 2002, and led the brand to customize the Ducati motorcycle itself the following year: a limited-edition 999R FILA, to celebrate the 200th victory in the Superbike World Championship.

IMAGE	PAGE(S)	YEAR	PRODUCT	DESIGNER	FEATURES
	–	2018	Jumper	Silvia Venturini Fendi	Long-sleeved white sweater with blue and red ribbing on the neckline, hem, and cuffs. What most characterizes the sweater is the logo embroidered in the center: Fendi Roma. The logo merges the graphic identities of two brands: Fendi's "F" reproduces the historic FILA logo, the F-Box, revealing the collaboration, unexpected and then immediately desired, presented for the first time in Milan on the catwalk of the Fendi Fall/Winter 2018 fashion show.
	–	2002	Shirt	–	Long-sleeved, bright red shirt with embroidered logos at chest height and on the sleeves. The shirt marks FILA's entry into the exciting world of Formula 1: it is in fact part of the uniform designed for the Ferrari team in 2002, the year in which FILA became Ferrari's official supplier of clothing, shoes, and accessories.
	203	1982	Tank top	FILA Design Team	White tank top with red profiles and F-Box logo embroidered on the bottom left. The tank top—an "underwear" garment that visually represents, in the collective imagination, a masculine Italian domesticity—becomes an item of clothing that can be worn outside, without inhibitions. The tank top is part of the Effe line, produced by FILA until 1982.
	203	1982	Tank top	FILA Design Team	White tank top with shaped armholes and F-Box logo embroidered on the bottom left. The garment is part of the Effe line, produced by FILA until 1982—a resilient testimony to the origins of the brand, which began with the production of yarns and subsequently of underwear knitwear at the beginning of the 1900s.
	–	1998	T-shirt	FILA Design Team	Short-sleeved T-shirt in hi-tech fabric with applied collar. The purple color and the lily printed on the left chest, opposite the FILA logo, placed on the right side at the same height, demonstrate the brand's interest in a beloved sport for all Italians: football. In 1998 FILA saw in the champion Gabriel Batistuta the incarnation of the spirit of the brand on the field, and decided to sponsor Florence's team Fiorentina, dressing the players from head to toe.
	217	2006	Sweatshirt	Gosha Rubchinskiy	Long-sleeved hooded sweatshirt, in the classic FILA colors—red, white, and blue—with logo in the center followed by Cyrillic writing. The writing is actually a signature: Gosha Rubchinskiy. The sweatshirt was presented by the Russian designer at Pitti Uomo in 2016, and became one of the symbols of his post-Soviet aesthetic, derived from the personal experience of the designer who grew up in Moscow, between local traditions and the Western influences released by the fall of the Berlin Wall and the dissolution of the Iron Curtain.
	–	2017	T-shirt	–	Blue V-neck T-shirt with short sleeves, sides marked by two red vertical lines and white polka dots of different sizes, and shoulders marked by horizontal red bands. The T-shirt features a "signature" printed in the center: that of Kim Clijsters, a Belgian athlete who announced her retirement in 2012, after having won 41 international titles. In 2017, FILA dedicated a special collection to Clijsters—of which this T-shirt is part—to celebrate the champion's entry into the International Tennis Hall of Fame.

IMAGE	PAGE(S)	YEAR	PRODUCT	DESIGNER	FEATURES
		1984	Jacket	Pierluigi Rolando	Jacket with Nehru collar, long sleeves, and central buttoning. The color is a bold light blue, with white horizontal lines on the sleeves and two embroidered logos: the Italian flag on the left and FILA on the right. The garment is part of the uniform that FILA designed to accompany the Italian national swimming team at the 1984 Los Angeles Olympics, during which FILA suits were on the podium, proudly worn by the athletes, 32 times.
		1984	K-Way	Pierluigi Rolando	K-Way in light blue waterproof hi-tech fabric, with long sleeves, hood, and contrasting white details. The Italian flag embroidered on the right chest contrasts with the FILA logo placed at the same height on the left. The colors and details characterize the collection to which the garment belongs: the official uniform for the swimmers of the Italian national team competing at the 1984 Los Angeles Olympics.
		1976	Sweater	Pierluigi Rolando	Turtleneck sweater in apple green yarn, with a cut at chest height that marks the bib in white yarn with blue vertical stripes of different sizes. The sweater has five press studs on the left side, which allow the neck to be opened. The colors reflect those of the mountain for which this sweater was designed: a garment that harmonizes the climber's body with the natural shades of the territory he explores. The respect that the item reserves for the mountain comes from the person who inspired and requested it: Reinhold Messner.
		1999	Tank top	FILA Design Team	Sleeveless blue tank top with V-neck trimmed in red. Red and white are the colors chosen for the details and logos, which identifies the garment as part of the official uniform of the Biella basketball team. Basketball is the discipline that exemplifies the rebirth of FILA in the 1990s and shepherded the arrival of the brand in new global scenarios. This garment demonstrates how attachment to the region of origin, to the roots, is always a source of great pride for FILA. Bonding with the local team and supporting its endeavors comes as a natural expression of this feeling.
	205	1973	Polo shirt	Pierluigi Rolando	Polo shirt in light fil d'Écosse, white with blue collar, green piping, and snap buttons. The polo shirt is one of the first objects that represents FILA's bond with the world of tennis. It belonged to Adriano Panatta, who wore it both on the court and for a famous shoot published in *L'Uomo Vogue*, transforming the champion into a style icon.
		1940	Girdle	FILA Design Team	Girdle made of lightweight wool. This is the oldest garment preserved in the FILA archive, dating back to around the 1940s: a precious testimony to the beginnings of the brand. FILA was founded in 1911 as a spinning mill. It then became a manufacturer of underwear, produced with circular knitwear machines. The revolution that would take FILA on its new course began in the 1960s, when the same circular machines were converted to produce all kinds of knitwear.
		1976	Sweatshirt	Pierluigi Rolando	White, blue, and red: three colors grace this sweatshirt with long sleeves and central zip. The sweatshirt is part of the "Pinguino," FILA's first tracksuit. The Pinguino was created to respond to the need for a "suit" that was not intended for the office but for leisure time: a moment to express individuality and also emulate idols. Elegance according to FILA. Pierluigi Rolando was inspired by the English Royal Guard for the cut and details, while the colors came from the style of penguins, naturally "wearing" tails. The Pinguino was proposed on the market as a "perfect" garment, a synthesis of classicism and the new, energetic push toward sport.

IMAGE	PAGE(S)	YEAR	PRODUCT	DESIGNER	FEATURES
	–	1992	T-shirt	–	White T-shirt with irregular black and white pattern, contrasting orange profile on the neckline, and FILA logo in acid green and orange. The T-shirt, worn by a very young Monica Seles, represents FILA's return to the tennis court. FILA had been designing its women's collection for Seles since 1988. Seles would also endorse FILA shoes; she was photographed in the famous 1992 campaign, which also features a quote from the athlete, embodying the spirit of the brand: "When your ambition drives you."
	–	1992	Polo shirt	–	White polo shirt with irregular purple graphic pattern and embroidered logos. The garment is part of the tennis collection from the early 1990s, endorsed by tennis player Monica Seles. The collection marked the brand's return to one of its most familiar courts, this time providing athletes with complete equipment, from polo shirts, dresses, and shorts to shoes, which the brand has invested in since the 1980s.
	67 (bottom left)	1975	Sweatshirt	Pierluigi Rolando	Sweatshirt with long sleeves and zip in the center, blue with contrasting white sides and inner sleeves, and white ribbed collar, bottom, and cuffs with black and red horizontal stripes. The sweatshirt—whose combination of colors was inspired by birds, real as well as mythological—is one of the color variants of the uniform worn by Björn Borg in the celebrations of victories on the most prestigious courts, in this case, Roland Garros. The two logos, F-Box and BJ, are placed side by side to declare that the brand dresses the icon and, in return, the icon represents the victorious identity of the brand.
	–	1999	Running ensemble	FILA Design Team	Yellow and light blue running ensemble consisting of a light tank top and a pair of shorts. The two pieces, seen together, seem to complement each other: the tank top has a light blue central body and yellow sides, and the shorts are in reverse colors. Among the different sports on which FILA focuses, running is the most cosmopolitan: FILA, in fact, dresses several international champions and teams. The first to wear a FILA running uniform was Moses Tanui, during the 1993 New York marathon.
	241–248	2000	Windbreaker	FILA Design Team	Windbreaker in bright yellow Gore-Tex hi-tech fabric. FILA experimented with materials and constructions for extreme environmental conditions in the 1970s, when the brand developed the five-pocket jacket made of "telavela" fabric, wind-resistant and with gussets on the sides. The research culminated in the collaboration with Giovanni Soldini for his epic undertaking, the Around Alone, in 1999. This jacket—made of sustainable materials and with flaps closed with Velcro—is the result of the observation of Soldini's movements: a uniform to respond to the unexpectedness of sea life.
	201	1978	Ski jacket	Pierluigi Rolando	Jacket with blue torso and bright yellow shoulders and sleeves. The colors relate the jacket to its wearer: Ingemar Stenmark, Swedish slalomist and first endorser of the FILA ski collection. How to protect the slalomist's arms from the plastic poles encountered during the descent? Starting from the equipment available at the time —wool sweaters with semi-rigid rubber ribs— and the study of other protective clothing such as riot jackets, Rolando designed plaques in the shape of the elements of the F-Box logo, made of aluminum with a rubber padding and bi-elastic plate. The result is a lightweight armor supporting the athlete in his race for victory.
	–	1981	Terrinda jacket	Pierluigi Rolando	Jacket with long sleeves and central zip closure, in bright blue with three thin white lines, one that crosses the jacket horizontally, from wrist to wrist, and two that run vertically on the right and left side. The jacket is called Terrinda, and is one of the most recognizable garments of the casual style typical of the 1980s, and a forerunner of athleisure-wear. The Terrinda was reissued in 2009, reproduced in a soft material, reminiscent of suede to the touch, in contrast with the proportions and lines of the details, from the collar to the angled pockets, inspired by biker clothing.

IMAGE	PAGE(S)	YEAR	PRODUCT	DESIGNER	FEATURES
	–	2009	Terrinda jacket	FILA Design Team	Jacket with long sleeves and central zip closure, white with three thin red lines, two placed vertically on the torso on the right and on the left, and one that connects the wrist. The suede-like material recalls the inspiration of the biker leather jacket, but translated into the FILA vocabulary, marrying comfort and style in everyday clothing. The garment is a Terrinda, a hybrid between sweatshirt and jacket, very popular in the 1980s, the decade in which it was presented on the market for the first time; it was then reproposed by FILA in the 2000s as a tribute to the historical identity of the brand.
	–	1993	Ski suit	FILA Design Team	Ski suit in stretch hi-tech fabric in various bright colors with black protections visible in the lower part of the trousers, from the knee down. The tracksuit is part of the collection created for the "valanga azzurra," the Italian ski team, and in particular for the spearhead of the team, Alberto Tomba. Its aggressive and bombastic style pushed FILA's researchers to work on cutting-edge materials, arriving at the production of a Carbon-Kevlar compound to protect the athlete's limbs from articulated slalom poles. Supported by his uniform, tailored to his needs, Tomba won the World Cup in 1995.
	–	1984	Sweatshirt	Pierluigi Rolando	Sweatshirt with long sleeves and central zip, high collar, and elastic band at the waist. The bright colors—blue, green, yellow, and white—are arranged in a clear but asymmetric geometry, and mitigated by the material chosen for the item: a soft velour, part of FILA's vocabulary since 1982, the year in which the FILA collection enhanced its offer, adding new shapes, tones, and materials, which would later become icons of the following decade.
	–	1976	Dress	Pierluigi Rolando	White dress with short sleeves and boat neckline marked by a blue border; the same border marks the beginning of the lower part of the dress: a pleated skirt with F-Box logo applied on the left. The dress is part of the famous FILA White Line: the line demonstrated awareness of the new fascination that sport exerted on society, and exploited the language of fashion to offer functional and desirable items, designed with tennis in mind but also appreciated for everyday life and style.
	194, 202, 233	1975	Sweatshirt	Pierluigi Rolando	Burgundy sweatshirt with long sleeves and zip in the center, featuring contrasting white sides and inner sleeves, and white ribbed collar, bottom, and cuffs with horizontal black and red stripes. The sweatshirt, elegant and measured in its proportions and color ratio, was made famous by Björn Borg, who wore it when he lifted the Wimbledon trophy in 1977. The sweatshirt bears two logos—F-Box and BJ—and exemplifies the shared intents between the brand and the champion: elegance and success.
	–	1982	Sweater	Pierluigi Rolando	Sweatshirt with long sleeves and zip, collar, and diagonal pockets. The dark blue color of the base is enriched by contrasting white details: the profiles of the pockets and a horizontal line that runs across the upper part of the torso. The left sleeve features the classic F-Box logo and two white bands right underneath it. The sweatshirt belongs to the White Line 1982 collection, which maintains the elegance as defined by the brand, updating it according to the new concept of leisure time that dominated the 1980s.

FILA: TIMELAPSE

Curated by
Angelo Flaccavento

Art Direction
Francesco Valtolina

Graphic Design
Francesco Valtolina
Nicola Narbone

Translations
Sylvia Adrian Notini

For the texts
Silvia Venturini Fendi
Marta Franceschini
Matteo Codignola
Carlo Antonelli
Emanuele Coccia
Michele Galluzzo
Lorenzo Ottone
Silvia Calderoni
Karl Holmqvist
Charlie Fox
Jeffrey Burton
Rahim Attarzadeh
CB Hoyo

Photo Editing
Marina Itolli

Photo Credits
All photos are courtesy of the Fondazione FILA Museum Archive.

© Giorgio Bertone: 109
© Carlo Borlenghi: 241–248
© Luciano Buglioni: 190
© Gianni Ciaccia / Agence Sport Vision: 119, 123, 124
© René Ghillini: 224
© Ray Giubilo: 135
© Sergio Goria / Fondazione FILA Museum Archive: 20 (right), 22 (right), 23–28, 30, 35–40, 42 (right), 46, 48 (right), 53, 54, 55, 57, 58, 59–91, 118, 141–148
© David M. Henschel: 97
© Čedomir Komljenović: 41, 42 (left), 163
© Reinhold Messner: 110, 171, 172, 174–178, 202
© Enrico Mininno: 20 (left), 24 (right), 33, 34 (left), 38 (right), 47, 48 (left), 63
© Dave Nagel / Nagel Photography: 112, 136
© Andreas Pollok: 181, 185
© Ricky Powell: 236
© Adam Pretty: 120
© Giancarlo Saliceti: 129
© Pietro Sthylla: 98, 126
© Angelo Tonelli: 102, 103, 115, 116
© Kazunori Tsukada: 225, 228, 229
© Zigen: 226, 234

The Publisher may be contacted by entitled parties for any iconographic sources that have not been identified.

© 2023 Mondadori Libri S.p.A.
Distributed in English throughout the World
by Rizzoli International Publications Inc.
300 Park Avenue South
New York, NY 10010, USA

ISBN: 978-88-918389-4-0

2024 2025 2026 2027 / 10 9 8 7 6 5 4 3 2 1

First edition: April 2024

All rights reserved. No part of this publication may be reproduced, stored in a retrieval system, or transmitted in any form or by any means, electronic, mechanical, photocopying, recording, or otherwise, without prior consent of the publishers.

This volume was printed
at O.G.M. SpA, Padova
Printed in Italy

Visit us online:
Facebook.com/RizzoliNewYork
Twitter: @Rizzoli_Books
Instagram.com/RizzoliBooks
Pinterest.com/RizzoliBooks
Youtube.com/user/RizzoliNY
Issuu.com/Rizzoli